The
Spirit
of Prayer

The
Spirit
of Prayer

*Selected and compiled by the author
from various portions of her works
exclusively on that subject*

by Hannah More

 CLARION CLASSICS
Zondervan Publishing House
Grand Rapids, Michigan

Clarion Classics are published by Zondervan Publishing House,
1415 Lake Drive, S.E., Grand Rapids, Michigan 49506

The Spirit of Prayer
Copyright © 1986 by The Zondervan Corporation
Grand Rapids, Michigan

Library of Congress Cataloging in Publication Data

More, Hannah, 1745–1833.
  The spirit of prayer.

  (Clarion classic)
  1. Prayer—Addresses, essays, lectures. I. Title.
BV213.M65   1986   248.3'2   86-1505
ISBN 0-310-43641-9

Designed by Ann Cherryman

Printed in the United States of America

86 87 88 89 90 / 10 9 8 7 6 5 4 3 2 1

Contents

Introduction

Marlene A. Hess

She fought for the slaves. She educated the poor. She warned the rich. She advised women. And she battled Thomas Paine and the atheistic radicals whose writings flooded England during the French Revolution. No class of people escaped her careful attention, especially when it came to moral and religious instruction. Hannah More (1745–1833) emerged as one of the great evangelical reformers of the eighteenth century. Most of her efforts came from her pen, and her writings quickly became bestsellers. Sometimes an entire edition of her books sold out within hours of publication.

Hannah More became a national figure. Her friends called her an Esther raised up to save her country, a Deborah to speak forth the truth of God. Charles Muir, in *Women: the Makers of History,* writes, "No woman ever made such a deep impression on the public mind or wielded such an influence as she did." It is difficult for us today to appreciate how the people of England idolized her while her fame spread to the United States and other parts of the world.

Hannah More's remarkable influence on English life began when she came from Bristol as a young woman and startled the fashionable London world with her witty conversation, clever poetry, and dramatic talent. With her sparkling personality she won the friendship of many important people. Samuel Johnson recited her own poetry to her, and the great Shakespearean actor, David Garrick, sponsored her drama *Percy,* which ran longer than any other play in the London theater of that year.

But just as her literary career was gaining momentum, she heard "the alarming call of God to Elijah" one night as she sat at the opera. "What doest thou here?" seemed to echo through her thoughts. Wanting to convert her time to "holy purposes," she withdrew from the London social scene and settled in rural Bristol with her four sisters.

Turning to moral and religious subjects, Hannah More became the foremost representative of evangelical Christianity in her country. Her association with the aristocrats paid off. In her books *Manners of the Great* and *Religion of the Fashionable World* she admonished the "good church people" of the upper crust, telling them that charity prompted by the desire for recognition and not for God was useless. "Christianity," she said, "is a religion of motives and principles." Always pointing to practical Christianity, she declared, "If Christ be a sacrifice for sin; let Him be also to us the example of an holy life." She urged the wealthy and influential to stand up as examples to the common people in their lives and habits. She radically proclaimed the equality of all people as sinners in need of salvation, whether rich or poor, king or farmer. Reproving society for its foibles and follies does not usually win bestseller awards, but Hannah More's works had an enormous circulation; most copies were snatched up within hours of publication. John Newton, the minister and hymn writer, told her that the Lord had allotted her "a post of great importance" for which "no person in the kingdom" had equal advantage.

Grateful for the reception of her books by the fashionable world, More turned her attention to the lower classes and applied her faith to actual practice. In doing so she gained an outstanding reputation as an educator and reformer. She had a good education and in her youth had taught in her sister's school in Bristol. After she moved to the country, she immediately noticed the poor in their "deplorable ignorance and depravity." When Hannah More visited Cheddar with William Wilberforce to see the Mendip Hills, the parliamentarian was so deeply moved by the poverty that he left his dinner untouched and thought of a plan to finance schools that Hannah More would start.

In canvassing the area, Hannah More found thirteen adjoining parishes without a single resident curate, and in one parish she saw only one Bible. It was used to prop up a flower pot!

The opposition to the schools was immense. But as Hannah traveled from village to village, she convinced the leaders that her instruction would not teach children to rob orchards but would instill in them good habits through learning the Scriptures. She followed the example of Robert Raikes in his Sunday schools, and at the end of a year she had five hundred children in schools in the Cheddar area. She also held evening readings of sermons, prayers, and hymns for the parents. Her schools grew to about seventeen hundred pupils in thirteen schools. Her yearly feasts attracted as many as five thousand onlookers alone.

In running her schools, Hannah More advocated "a suitable education for each and a Christian education for all." She put the royalties from her writings into her schools, and her work aroused so much sympathy in England that people everywhere offered money to endow charities to help alleviate suffering caused by poverty.

Nothing deterred Hannah More from her good works. She would help anyone, from peasants to peers, from priests to profligates. When she was not writing against "the impious and detestable practice of duelling" or slavery, that "opprobrious traffic in the human species," she would come to the aid of Catholic priests who had fled from the French Revolution or she would search out the flophouses for a young girl who had been abducted.

Among the unlikely recipients of Hannah More's care and concern were a madwoman, the Lady of the Haystack, and a woman of loose morals who had thrown herself into the river. Hannah More set out immediately to "see what could be done." She traced the girl to "a street of very bad fame," learned how her father had "sold her at sixteen in the King's Bench to a fellow prisoner," and persuaded her to leave the unfaithful "protector," whose neglect had driven her to attempt suicide. Unfortunately, the girl did not follow the advice. Yet Hannah More would gladly receive her back if "it should please God to touch her heart with true repentance." Her whole tone toward unfortunates was pity, not blame. Always she did as much as she could, and when her efforts ended in vain, she accepted failure without any reproach.

For the poor, Hannah More went more than the second mile, even if it meant corrupting her elegant and polished writing style. When revolutionary activity came spilling over from France in the form of "inflammatory publications," letters began pouring in to More "by every post, from persons of eminence, earnestly calling upon her to produce some little popular tract which might serve as a counteraction to those pernicious writings." At first she refused. But when her friend Bishop Porteus of London persuaded her to write an antidote to Thomas Paine's *Rights of Man*, she consented, saying, "Against my will and judgment, on one sick day I scribbled a little pamphlet." She called it "vulgar as heart can wish" and "repugnant" to her nature, yet the tract proved extremely popular. Titled *Village Politics*, it introduced Edmund Burke's philosophy in a popular vein by having lively dialogue between Will Chip and a radical Paine convert.

This tract paved the way for the monumental effort of the *Cheap Repository Tracts*, underwritten by the evangelical Clapham group. Hannah More shrewdly observed in her schools that "to teach the poor to *read*, without providing them with *safe*" books was "dangerous." For three years she launched her series of moral tales, ballads, and special Sunday readings of sermons, prayers, and Bible stories aimed at offsetting the influence of vicious broadsides and chapbooks hawked by peddlers and popular with the semi-literate. Even though the tracts were written for the poor, they reached every corner of England, had a large circulation in the United States, and were translated into several languages. Three hundred thousand were sold between March 3 and April 18. One year later two million had been sold—a record in publishing history for that time!

Full of vigor and entertainment, the little tales portrayed colorful village characters speaking lively dialogue and illustrating moral lessons. Among the shopkeepers, the baker, the blacksmith, the farmer, was Black Giles the rat-catcher. His wife, Tawney Rachel, tramped the roads with a basket on her arm pretending to sell laces, cabbage nets, and chapbooks, but her true profession was telling fortunes and thieving.

The Shepherd of Salisbury Plain is More's most famous tract and was described by F. K. Brown as "a flawless masterpiece perfect in conception and in execution, likely to remain forever peerless on a height the moral tale will not reach again." The contentment of the shepherd in the most deprived circumstances and his simple faith in God inspire the reader and offer a Christlike example to those in unfortunate circumstances.

Hannah More joined the evangelicals at the forefront of the battle against slavery in Great Britain. When Wilberforce tried for the first time to present the Bill for the Abolition of the Slave Trade in the House of Commons, Hannah More was asked to write poetry to win public opinion against slavery. *The Slave Trade* is a passionate expression of feelings toward the plight of the slaves. Again she pointed to the equality of all people because all are made in the image of God.

Another area of equality Hannah More urged was in women's education. She was ahead of her time in saying that God made man and woman of one flesh and that there was no fundamental inferiority or superiority between them. She disavowed radical feminist attitudes but pushed for moderate reforms for women. In her *Strictures on the Modern System of Female Education* (1799), she stressed Christian education for the minds as well as the souls of girls. This bestseller won her so much respect for her ideas that the Queen of England asked her to write a book for the education of the princess. This she did and included much on the Christian life.

Hannah More's most famous work was *Coelebs in Search of a Wife*. This evangelical novel won the attention of every literary periodical of the time. Although most of the reviews were favorable, they criticized her for her severe attitude toward amusements and her insistence on the doctrine of total depravity. But Hannah More always wrote for a purpose. Just as she seized upon fiction as a vehicle for moral and religious instruction in her *Cheap Repository* for the poor, so she took up the novel to speak to the middle-class patrons of the circulating libraries. She had been adamantly opposed to novels, saying they were frivolous at best and morally damaging at worst. But because she tried to provide an "antidote for the poison of novels," she countered with an ideal pattern of Christian marriage and family life. The hero goes from one family to another among his acquaintances, looking for the right wife. The book "swept through the land with the force of a tornado," wrote W. P. Courtney. Thirty thousand copies were sold in America alone.

Toward the end of her long life, as ill health plagued her, Hannah More continued her ministry of writing. Upon the abolition of slavery in Ceylon, she wrote a poetical dialogue, *The Feast of Freedom.* Charles Wesley set it to music, and it was publicly performed in Cingalese.

Her last work, *The Spirit of Prayer,* she compiled from earlier writings and published in 1825 when she was eighty. Her whole argument for prayer in this book rests on her central belief in the fall of man. She asserts that we are all sinners; we are all helpless; and this knowledge "drives us out of ourselves in search of divine assistance." In her typically balanced style and gentle approach to great issues, she reminds us that while we keep our own corruption in view, "let us look with equal intentness on that mercy which cleanseth from all sin." This keen awareness of man's sinful condition and God's grace was what drove Hannah More to serve others with such compassion and fervency.

Preface

Knowing that shortly I must put off this my tabernacle. I will endeavor that you may be able after my decease to have these things always in remembrance.

—2 Peter 1:14–15.

From a sick and, in all human probability, a dying bed, the writer of these pages feels an earnest desire to be enabled, with the blessing of God, to execute a little plan which has at different times crossed her mind, but which she never found leisure to accomplish till the present season of incapacity.

"The importunity of friends," that hackneyed apology for works of inferior merit, is not in the present instance the less true for being worn threadbare. By many partial friends she has frequently been desired to write a volume exclusively on Prayer. With this request she has always declined complying, because, among other reasons, she was aware that she had previously exhausted not the subject itself, which is indeed inexhaustible, but the slender resources of her own mind.

In her perhaps too numerous printed works, written on different subjects and at distant periods, there are very many volumes in which not only some reference has been made, but some distinct portions assigned to the all-important subject of Prayer.

It is now her latest and warmest wish to be permitted to collect and examine some of those portions which treat more directly of this great duty; to unite the scattered members into one compact body; and to bring each under its proper head, into one point of view. All she is herself able to do is to hear these extracts read by kind friends and to adopt such passages as she may think proper for selection.

Perhaps the silence and solitude of her present nightly watchings may, through divine grace, impress her own heart with a still deeper sense of the unspeakable importance and value of Prayer, and of the support and consolation which may be granted in answer to this exercise, when every other support and consolation must inevitably fail.

However small may be the use of the compilation to the reader, the writer at least is already reaping one benefit herself from what she has presumed to suggest to others: the benefit of feeling, as she reviews these pages, how sadly she herself has fallen short in the duties she has so repeatedly recommended. In this re-examination she has sensibly felt how easy it is to be good upon paper and how difficult in practice.

At the same time she humbly trusts that her very failures may have enabled her to touch these subjects more experimentally than she might have done had her own deficiencies been less powerfully recollected and less acutely felt.

The Author ventures to hope that her valued friends, to whom this selection is more especially dedicated, will consider it as the last bequest of one who, about to quit this transitory scene and feeling the deepest interest in their spiritual prosperity, as also for that of all her fellow Christians, is desirous, by this her final act, to testify at least her affectionate anxiety for their eternal happiness.

The present weak state of the Author must apologize for inaccuracies and repetitions.

Chapter I

The Necessity of Prayer Founded on the Corruption of Human Nature

The subject of man's apostasy is so nearly connected with the subject of Prayer, being indeed that which constitutes the necessity of this duty, that some mention of the one ought to precede any discussion of the other. Let, then, the conviction that we have fallen from our original state, and that this lapse presents the most powerful incentive to prayer, furnish an apology for making a few preliminary remarks on this great article of our faith.

The doctrine is not the less a fundamental doctrine because it has been abused to the worst purposes, some having erroneously considered it as leaving us without hope, and others as leaving an excuse to unresisted sin. It is a doctrine which meets us in one unbroken series throughout the whole sacred volume. We find it from the third of Genesis, which records the event of man's apostasy, carried on through the history of its fatal consequences in all the subsequent instances of sin, individual and national, and running in one continued stream from the first sad tale of woe to the close of the sacred canon in the Apocalyptic Vision.

And to remove the groundless hope that this quality of inherent corruption belonged only to the profligate and abandoned, the divine Inspirer of the sacred writers took especial care that they should not confine themselves to relate the sins of these alone.

Why are the errors, the weaknesses, and even the crimes of the best of men recorded with equal fidelity? Why are we told of the twice repeated deceit of the father of the faithful? Why of the single instance of vanity in Hezekiah? Why of the too impetuous zeal of Elijah? Why of the error of the almost perfect Moses? Why of the insincerity of Jacob? Why of the far darker crimes of the otherwise holy David? Why of the departure of the wisest of men from that piety displayed with sublimity unparalleled in the dedication of the Temple? Why seems it to have been invariably studied to record with more minute detail the vices and errors of these eminent men than even those of the successive impious kings of Israel and of Judah, while these last are generally dismissed with the brief, but melancholy sentence that they did that which was evil in the sight of the Lord, followed only by too frequent an intimation that they made way for a successor worse than themselves? The answer is that the truth of our universal lapse could only be proved by transmitting the record of those vices from which even the holiest men were not exempt.

Had the Holy Scriptures kept back from man the faithful delineations of the illustrious characters to which we have referred, the truth of the doctrine in question, though occasionally felt, and in spite of his resistance, forced upon him, would not have been believed; or, if believed, would not have been acknowledged.

Christianity hangs on a few plain truths: "that God is, and that He is the rewarder of all that seek Him"; that man has apostatized from his original character, and by it has forfeited his original destination; that Christ came into this world and died upon the cross to expiate sin and to save sinners; that after His ascension into heaven, He did not leave His work imperfect. He sent His Holy Spirit, who performed His first office by giving to the apostles miraculous powers. His offices did not cease there. He has indeed withdrawn His miraculous gifts, but He still continues His silent but powerful operations, and that in their due order:

first, that of convincing of sin and of changing the heart of the sinner before he assumes the gracious character of the Comforter. What need, then, of heresies to perplex doctrines or of philosophy to entangle or of will-worshippers to multiply them?

We do not deny that there are in Christianity high and holy mysteries, but these "secret things," though they "belong to God," have their practical uses for us: They teach us humility, the prime Christian grace; they send us to prayer; and they exercise faith, the parent attribute of all other graces.

This religion of facts, then, the poorest listeners in the aisles of our churches understand sufficiently to be made by it wise unto salvation. They are saved by a practical belief of a few simple but inestimable truths.

By these same simple truths, martyrs and confessors, our persecuted saints and our blessed reformers were saved. By these few simple truths, Locke and Boyle and Newton were saved; not because they saw their religion through the glass of their philosophy, but because theirs was not a "philosophy, falsely so called"; nor their science, "a science of opposition," but a science and a philosophy which were made subservient to Christianity, and because their deep humility sanctified their astonishing powers of mind. These wonderful men, at whose feet the learned world is still satisfied to sit, sat themselves at the feet of Jesus. Had there been any other way but the cross by which sinners could be saved, they, perhaps of all men, were best qualified to have found it.

To return, then, to the particular doctrine under consideration: Let us believe man is corrupt because the Bible tells us he is so. Let us believe that all were so by nature, even the best, since we learn it from divine authority. Let us, from the same authority, trace the disorder to its source from a fallen parent, its seat in a corrupt heart, its extent through the whole man, its universality over the entire race.

All are willing to allow that we are subject to frailties, to imperfections, to infirmities. Facts compel us to confess a propensity to crimes, but worldly men confine the commission of them to the vulgar. But to rest here would lead us to a very false estimate of the doctrine in question, contrary to the decisive language of Scripture. It would establish corruption to be an accident and not a root. It would, by a division of offenders into two classes, deny that all offenses are derived from one common principle.

If, then, men would examine their own bosoms as closely as they censure the faults of others loudly, we should all find there the incipient stirrings of many a sin, which, when brought into action by circumstances, produce consequences the most appalling. Let us then bless God, not that we are better than other men, but that we are placed by Providence out of the reach of being goaded by that temptation, stimulated by that poverty, which, had they been our lot, might have led to the same termination.

Let, then, the fear of God, the knowledge of His Word, and the knowledge of ourselves teach us that there is not by nature so wide a difference between ourselves and others as we fondly imagine, that there is not by nature a great gulf fixed, that they who are on this side might not pass over to the other. Let us not look to any superior virtue, to any native strength of our own. But let us look with a lively gratitude to that mercy of God which has preserved us from the temptations to which they have yielded. But above all, let us look to that preventing and restraining grace which is withheld from none who ask it. Without this all-powerful grace, Latimer might have led Bonner to the stake; with it Bonner might have ascended the scaffold a martyr to true religion. Without this grace, Luther might have fattened on the sale of indulgences, and with it Leo the Tenth might have accomplished the blessed work of Reformation.

Chapter II

The Duty of Prayer Inferred From the Helplessness of Man

Man is not only a sinful, he is also a helpless and therefore a dependent being. This offers new and powerful motives for the necessity of prayer, the necessity of looking continually to a higher power, to a better strength than our own. If that Power sustain us not, we fall. If He direct us not, we wander. His guidance is not only perfect freedom, but perfect safety. Our greatest danger begins from the moment we imagine we are able to go alone.

The self-sufficiency of man, arising from his imaginary dignity, is a favorite doctrine with the nominal Christian. He feeds his pride with this pernicious aliment. And, as we hear much, so we hear falsely of the dignity of human nature. Prayer, founded on the true principles of Scripture, alone teaches us wherein our true dignity consists. The dignity of a fallen creature is a perfect anomaly. True dignity, contrary to the common opinion that it is an inherent excellence, is actually a sense of the want of it. It consists not in our valuing ourselves, but in a continual feeling of our dependence upon God and an unceasing aim at conformity to His image.

Nothing but a humbling sense of the sinfulness of our nature, of our practiced offenses, of our utter helplessness and constant dependence can bring us to fervent and persevering prayer. How did the faith of the saints of old flourish under a darker dispensation, through all the clouds and ignorance which obscured their views of God? "They looked unto Him, and were enlightened!" How their slender means and high attainments reproach us!

David found that the strength and spirit of nature, which had enabled him to resist the lion and the bear, did not enable him to resist his outward temptations, nor to conquer his inward corruptions. He therefore prayed not only for deliverance "from blood-guiltiness" for a grievously remembered sin; he prayed for the *principle* of piety, for the *fountain* of holiness, for "the creation of a clean heart," for "the renewing of a right spirit," for "truth in the inward parts," that the "comfort of God's help might be granted him." This uniform avowal of the secret workings of sin, this uniform dependence on the mercy of God to pardon and the grace of God to assist, render his precatory addresses, though they are those of a sovereign and a warrior, so universally applicable to the case of every private Christian.

One of our best poets (himself an unsuccessful courtier), from a personal experience of the mortifying feelings of abject solicitation, has said that if there were the man in the world whom he was at liberty to hate, he would wish him no greater punishment than *attendance* and *dependence.* But he applies the heavy penalty of this wish to the dependants on *mortal* greatness.

Now, attendance and dependence are the very essence both of the safety and happiness of a Christian. Dependence on God is his only true liberty, as attendance on Him is his only true consolation. The suitor for human favor is liable to continual disappointment. If he knocks at the door of his patron, there is probably a general order not to admit him. In the higher case, there is a special promise that "to him that knocks it shall be opened." The human patron hates importunity; the heavenly Patron invites it. The one receives his suitor according to his humor or refuses his admission from the caprice of the moment. With the other "there is no variableness, nor shadow of turning." "Come unto me," is His uniform invitation. The Almighty donor never puts off

His humble petitioner to a more convenient season. *His* Court of Requests is always open. He receives the petition as soon as it is offered. He grants it as soon as it is made. And though He will not dispense with a continuance of the application, yet to every fresh application He promises fresh support. He will still be solicited, but it is in order that He may still bestow. Repeated gifts do not exhaust His bounty, nor lessen His power of fulfillment. Repeated solicitation, so far from wearing His patience, is an additional call for His favor.

Nor is the lateness of the petition any bar to its acceptance. He likes that it should be early, but He rejects it not though it be late.

And as past mercies on God's part, so, to the praise of His grace, be it said that past offenses on our own part are no hindrance to the application of hearty repentance or the answer of fervent prayer.

The man in power has many claimants on his favor and comparatively few boons to bestow. The God of Power has all things in His gift and only blames the solicitor for coming so seldom or coming so late or staying so little a while. He only wishes that His best gifts were more earnestly sought.

When we solicit an earthly benefactor, it is often upon the strength of some pretense of his favor, the hope of some reward for past services. Even if we can produce little claim, we insinuate something like merit. But when we approach our Heavenly Benefactor, so far from having any thing like claim, any thing like merit to produce, our only true and our only acceptable plea is our utter want both of claim and merit—the utter destitution of all that can recommend us. Yet we presume to ask favor when we deserve nothing but rejection. We are encouraged to ask for eternal happiness when we deserve only eternal punishment. Though we have nothing to produce but disloyalty, we ask for the privileges of subjects; though nothing but disobedience to offer, we plead the privileges of children; we implore the tenderness of a father.

The petitioner to human power who may formerly have offended his benefactor contrives to soften his displeasure by representing that the offense was a small one. The devout petitioner to God uses no such subterfuge. In the boldness of faith and the humility of repentance, he cries, "Pardon my iniquity, for it is *great.*"

He who does not believe this fundamental truth, "the helplessness of man," on which the other doctrines of the Bible are built—even he who does nominally profess to assent to it as a doctrine of Scripture, yet if he does not experimentally acknowledge it, if he does not feel it in the convictions of his own awakened conscience, in his discovery of the evil workings of his own heart and the wrong propensities of his own nature, all bearing their testimony to its truth—such a one will not pray earnestly for its cure, will not pray with that feeling of his helplessness with that sense of dependence on divine assistance which alone makes prayer efficacious.

Of this corruption he can never attain an adequate conception till his progress in religion has opened his eyes on what is the natural state of man. Till this was the case, he himself was as far from desiring the change as he was from believing it necessary. He does not even suspect its existence till he is in some measure delivered from its dominion.

Nothing will make us truly humble, nothing will make us constantly vigilant, nothing will entirely lead us to have recourse to prayer, so fervently or so frequently, as this ever-abiding sense of our corrupt and helpless nature, as our not being able to ascribe any disposition in ourselves to anything that is good or any power to avoid, by our own strength, anything that is evil.

Chapter III

Prayer: Its Definition

Prayer is the application of want to Him who alone can relieve it, the voice of sin to Him who alone can pardon it. It is the urgency of poverty, the prostration of humility, the fervency of penitence, the confidence of trust. It is not eloquence, but earnestness; not figures of speech, but compunctions of soul. It is the "Lord save us, we perish" of drowning Peter; the cry of faith to the ear of mercy.

Adoration is the noblest employment of created beings; confession, the natural language of guilty creatures; praise, the spontaneous expression of pardoned sinners. Prayer is desire, the abasement of contrition, the energy of gratitude. It is not a mere conception of the mind, nor an effort of the intellect, nor an act of the memory, but an elevation of the soul toward its Maker. It is the devout breathing of a creature struck with a sense of its own misery and of the infinite holiness of Him whom it is addressing, experimentally convinced of its own emptiness and of the abundant fullness of God, of His readiness to hear, of His power to help, of His willingness to save. It is not an emotion produced in the senses, nor an effect wrought by the imagination, but a determination of the will, an effusion of the heart.

Prayer is the guide to self-knowledge by prompting us to look after our sins in order to pray against them. It is a motive to vigilance by teaching us to guard against those sins which, through self-examination, we have been enabled to detect.

Prayer is an act both of the understanding and of the heart. The understanding must apply itself to the knowledge of the divine perfections, or the heart will not be led to the adoration of them. It would not be a *reasonable* service if the mind was excluded. It must be rational worship, or the human worshiper would not bring to the service the distinguishing faculty of his nature, which is reason. It must be spiritual worship, or it would want the distinctive quality to make it acceptable to Him who is a spirit and who has declared that He will be worshiped "in spirit and in truth."

Prayer is right in itself as the most powerful means of resisting sin and advancing in holiness. It is above all right, as everything is which has the authority of Scripture, the command of God, and the example of Christ.

There is a perfect consistency in all the ordinations of God, a perfect congruity in the whole scheme of His dispensations. If man were not a corrupt creature, such prayer as the Gospel enjoins would not have been necessary. Had not prayer been an important means for curing those corruptions, a God of perfect wisdom would not have ordered it. He would not have prohibited everything which tends to inflame and promote them, had they not existed; nor would He have commanded everything that has a tendency to diminish and remove them, had not their existence been fatal. Prayer, therefore, is an indispensable part of His economy and of our obedience.

It is a hackneyed objection to the use of prayer that it is offending the omniscience of God to suppose He requires information of our wants. But no objection can be more futile. We do not pray to inform God of our wants, but to express our sense of the wants which He already knows. As He has not so much made His promises to our necessities as to our requests should be made before we can hope that our necessities will be relieved. God does not promise to those who want that they shall "have," but to those who "ask"; nor to those who need that they shall "find," but to those who "seek." So far, therefore, from His previous knowledge of our wants being a ground of objection to prayer, it is, in fact, the true ground for our application. Were He not Knowledge itself, our information would be of as little use as our application would be, were He not Goodness itself.

We cannot attain to a just notion of prayer while we remain ignorant of our own nature, of the nature of God as revealed in Scripture, of our relation to Him and dependence on Him. If, therefore, we do not live in the daily study of the Holy Scriptures, we shall want the highest motives to this duty and the best helps for performing it. If we do, the cogency of these motives and the inestimable value of these helps will render argument unnecessary and exhortation superfluous.

One cause, therefore, of the dullness of many Christians in prayer is their slight acquaintance with the sacred volume. They hear it periodically. They read it occasionally. They are contented to know it historically, to consider it superficially. But they do not endeavor to get their minds imbued with its spirit. If they store their memory with its facts, they do not impress their hearts with its truths. They do not regard it as the nutriment on which their spiritual life and growth depend. They do not pray over it. They do not consider all its doctrines as of practical application. They do not cultivate that spiritual discernment which alone can enable them judiciously to appropriate its promises and apply its denunciations to their own actual case. They do not use it as an unerring line to ascertain their own rectitude or detect their own obliquities.

In our retirements we too often fritter away our precious moments (moments rescued from the world) in trivial, sometimes, it is to be feared, in corrupt thoughts. But if we must give the reins to our imagination, let us send this excursive faculty to range among great and noble objects. Let it stretch forward, under the sanction of faith and the anticipation of prophecy, to the accomplishment of those glorious promises and tremendous threatenings which will soon be realized in the eternal world. These are topics which, under the safe and sober guidance of Scripture, will fix its largest speculations and sustain its loftiest flights. The same Scripture, while it expands and elevates the mind, will keep it subject to the dominion of truth; while at the same time it will teach it that its boldest excursions must fall infinitely short of the astonishing realities of a future state.

Though we cannot pray with a too deep sense of sin, we may make our sins too exclusively the object of our prayers. While we keep, with a self-abasing eye, our own corruptions in view, let us look with equal intentness on that mercy which cleanseth from all sin. Let our prayers be all humiliation, but let them not be all complaint. When men indulge no other thought but that they are tainted rebels, the hopelessness of pardon hardens them into disloyalty. Let them look to the mercy of the King as well as to the rebellion of the subject. If we contemplate His grace as displayed in the Gospel, then, though our humility will increase, our despair will vanish. Gratitude in this, as in human instances, will create affection: "We love Him because He first loved us."

Let us, therefore, always keep our unworthiness in view, as a reason why we stand in need of the mercy of God in Christ, but never plead it as a reason why we should not draw nigh to Him to implore that mercy. The best men are unworthy for their own sakes; the worst, on repentance, will be accepted for His sake and through His merits.

In prayer, then, the perfections of God, and especially His mercies in our redemption, should occupy our thoughts as much as our sins; our obligations to Him as much as our departures from Him. We should keep up in our hearts a constant sense of our own weakness, not with a design to discourage the mind and depress the spirits, but with a view to drive us out of ourselves in search of the divine assistance. We should contemplate our infirmity in order to draw us to look for His strength and to seek that power from God which we vainly look for in ourselves. We do not tell a sick friend of his danger in order to grieve or terrify him, but to induce him to apply to his physician and to have recourse to his remedy.

Among the charges which have been brought against serious piety, one is that it teaches men to despair. The charge is just, in one sense, as to the fact, but false in the sense intended. It teaches us to despair, indeed, of ourselves, while it inculcates that faith in a Redeemer which is the true antidote to despair. Faith quickens the doubting, while it humbles the presumptuous spirit. The lowly Christian takes comfort in the blessed promise that God will never forsake them that are his. The presumptuous man is equally right in the doctrine but wrong in applying it. He takes that comfort to himself which was meant for another class of characters. The misappropriation of Scripture's promises and threatenings is the cause of much error and delusion.

Some devout enthusiasts have fallen into error by an unnatural and impracticable disinterestedness, asserting that God is to be loved exclusively for Himself, with an absolute renunciation of any view of advantage to ourselves. Yet that prayer cannot be mercenary which involves God's glory with our own happiness and makes His will the law of our requests. Though we are to desire the glory of God supremely, though this ought to be our grand actuating principle, yet He has graciously permitted, commanded, invited us to attach our own happiness to this primary object. The Bible exhibits not only a beautiful, but an inseparable combination of both, which delivers us from the danger of preposterously imagining that an absolute renunciation of all benefit to ourselves is necessary for the promotion of God's glory on the one hand, and on the other, from seeking any happiness independent of Him and underived from Him. In enjoining us to love Him supremely, He has connected an unspeakable blessing with a paramount duty, the highest privilege with the most positive command.

What a triumph for the humble Christian to be assured that "the everlasting God, the Lord, the Creator of the ends of the earth" is the God of his life, to know that he is even invited to take the Lord for his God. To close with God's offers, to accept His invitations, to receive God as our portion must surely be more pleasing to our heavenly Father than separating our happiness from His glory. To disconnect our interests from His goodness is at once to detract from His perfections and to obscure the brightness of our own hopes. The declarations of the inspired writers are confirmed by the authority of the heavenly hosts. They proclaim that the glory of God and the happiness of His creatures, so far from interfering, are connected with each other. We know but of one anthem composed and sung by angels, and this most harmoniously combines "the glory of God in the highest, with peace on earth, and good will to men."

"The beauty of Scripture," says the great Saxon reformer, "consists in pronouns." This God is *our* God. God, even our *own* God, shall bless us. How delightful the appropriation to glorify Him as being in Himself consummate excellence and to love Him from the feeling that His excellence is directed to our felicity! Here modesty would be ingratitude, disinterestedness rebellion. It would be severing ourselves from Him in whom we live and move and are. It would be dissolving the astonishing connection which He had condescended to establish between Himself and His rational creatures.

The Scripture saints make this union the chief ground of their grateful exultation: "*My* strength," "*my* rock," "*my* fortress," "*my* deliverer!" Again, "let the God of *my* salvation be exalted"! Now take away the pronoun and substitute the article *the*, how comparatively cold is the impression! The consummation of the joy arises from the peculiarity, the intimacy, the endearment of the relation.

Nor to the liberal Christian is the grateful joy diminished when he blesses his God as "the God of them that trust in Him." All general blessings, will he say, all providential mercies are mine individually, are mine as completely as if no other shared in the enjoyment—life, light, the earth and heavens, the sun and stars, whatsoever sustains the body, and recreates the spirits. My obligation is as great as if the mercy had been made purely for me. As great? Nay, it is greater. It is augmented by a sense of the millions who participate in the blessing. The same enlargement of personal obligation holds good, nay, rises higher, in the mercies of Redemption. The Lord is *my* Savior as completely as if He had redeemed only me. That He has redeemed "a great multitude, which no man can number, of all nations, and kindreds, and people, and tongues" is diffusion without abatement; it is general participation without individual diminution. Each has all.

In adoring the providence of God, we are apt to be struck with what is new and out of course, while we too much overlook long habitual and uninterrupted mercies. But common mercies, if less striking, are more valuable, both because we have them always and, for the reason above assigned, because others share them. The ordinary blessings of life are overlooked for the very reason that they ought to be most prized: because they are most uniformly bestowed. They are most essential to our support, and when once they are withdrawn, we begin to find that they are also most essential to our comfort. Nothing raises the pride of a blessing like its removal, whereas it was its continuance which should have taught us its worth. We require novelties to awaken our gratitude, not considering that it is the duration of mercies which enhances their value. We want fresh excitements. We consider mercies long enjoyed as things of course, as things to which we have a sort of claim by prescription, as if God had no right to withdraw what He has once bestowed, as if He were obliged to continue what He has once been pleased to confer.

But that the sun has shone unremittingly from the day that God created him is not a less stupendous exertion of power than that the hand which fixed him in the heavens and marked out his progress through them once said by His servant, "Sun, stand thou still upon Gideon." That he has gone on in his strength, driving his uninterrupted career and "rejoicing as a giant to run his course" for six thousand years is a more astonishing exhibition of Omnipotence than that he should have been once suspended by the hand which set him in motion. That the ordinances of heaven, that the established laws of nature should have been for one day interrupted to serve a particular occasion, is a less real wonder, and certainly a less substantial blessing, than that in such a multitude of ages they should have pursued their appointed course for the comfort of the whole system.

As the affections of the Christian ought to be set on things above, so it is for them that his prayers will be chiefly addressed. God, in promising to "give those who delight in Him the desire of their heart," could never mean temporal things; for these they might desire improperly as to the object and inordinately as to the degree. The promise relates principally to spiritual blessings. He not only gives us these mercies, but the very desire to obtain them is also His gift. Here our prayer requires no qualifying, no conditioning, no limitation. We cannot err in our choice, for God Himself is the object of it. We cannot exceed in the degree unless it were possible to love Him too well or to please Him too much.

God shows His munificence in encouraging us to ask most earnestly for the greatest things, by promising that the smaller "shall be added unto us." We therefore acknowledge His liberality most when we request the highest favors. He manifests His infinite superiority to earthly fathers by chiefly delighting to confer those spiritual gifts which *they* less solicitously desire for their children than those worldly advantages on which God sets so little value.

We should endeavor to render our private devotions effectual remedies for our own particular sins. Prayer against sin, in general, is too indefinite to reach the individual case. We must bring it home to our own hearts, else we may be confessing another man's sins and overlooking our own. If we have any predominant fault, we should pray more especially against the fault. If we pray for any virtue of which we particularly stand in need, we should dwell on our own deficiencies in that virtue till our souls become deeply affected with our want of it. Our prayers should be circumstantial, not as was before observed, for the information of Infinite Wisdom, but for the stirring up of our own dull affections. And as the recapitulation of our wants tends to keep up a sense of our dependence, the enlarging on our especial mercies will tend to keep alive a sense of gratitude; while indiscriminate petitions, confessions, and thanksgiving leave the mind to wander in indefinite devotion and unaffecting generalities, without personality, and without appropriation. It must be obvious that we except the so grand universal points in which all have an equal interest, and which must always form the essence of family, and especially, of public prayer.

As we ought to live in a spirit of obedience to His commands, so we should live in a frame of waiting for His blessings on our prayers and in a spirit of gratitude when we have obtained it. This is that "preparation of the heart" which would always keep us in a posture for duty. If we desert the duty because an immediate blessing does not visibly attend it, it shows that we do not serve God out of conscience, but selfishness; that we grudge expending on Him that service which brings us in no immediate interest. Though He grants not our petition, let us never be tempted to withdraw our application.

Our reluctant devotions may remind us of the remark of a certain great political wit,* who apologized for his late attendance in parliament by his being detained while a party of soldiers were *dragging a volunteer* to his duty. How many excuses do we find for not being in time! How many apologies for brevity! How many evasions for neglect! How unwilling, too often, are we to come into the divine presence! How reluctant to remain in it! Those hours which are least valuable for business, which are least seasonable for pleasure, we commonly give to religion. Our energies, which were so readily exerted in the society we have just quitted, are sunk as we approach the divine presence. Our hearts, which were all alacrity in some frivolous conversation, become cold and inanimate, as if it were the natural property of devotion to freeze the affections. Our animal spirits, which so readily performed their functions before, now slacken their vigor and lose their vivacity. The sluggish body sympathizes with the unwilling mind, and each promotes the deadness of the other; both are slow in listening to the call of duty; both are soon weary in performing it. How do our fancies rove back to the pleasures

*Mr. Sheridan.

we have been enjoying! How apt are the diversified images of those pleasures to mix themselves with our better thoughts, to pull down our high aspirations! As prayer requires all the energies of the compound being of man, so we too often feel as if there were a confederacy of body, soul, and spirit to disincline and disqualify us for it.

When the heart is once sincerely turned to religion, we need not, every time we pray, examine into every truth and seek for conviction over and over again, but assume that those doctrines are true, the truth of which we have already proved. From a general and fixed impression of these principles will result a taste, a disposedness, a love so intimate that the convictions of the understanding will become the affections of the heart.

To be deeply impressed with a few fundamental truths, to digest them thoroughly, to meditate on them seriously, to pray over them fervently, to get them deeply rooted in the heart will be more productive of faith and holiness than to labor after variety, ingenuity, or elegance. The indulgence of imagination will rather distract than edify. Searching after ingenious thoughts will rather divert the attention from God to ourselves than promote fixedness of thought, singleness of intention, and devotedness of spirit. Whatever is subtle and refined is in danger of being unscriptural. If we do not guard the mind, it will learn to set more value on original thoughts than devout affections. It is the business of prayer to cast down imaginations which gratify the natural activity of the mind, while they leave the heart unhumbled.

We should confine ourselves to the present business of the present moment. We should keep the mind in a state of perpetual dependence. We should entertain no long views. "*Now* is the accepted time." "Today we must hear His voice." "Give us *this* day our daily bread." The manna will not keep till tomorrow. Tomorrow will have its own wants and must have its own petitions. Tomorrow we must seek anew the bread of heaven.

We should, however, avoid coming to our devotions with unfurnished minds. We should be always laying in materials for prayer by a diligent course of serious reading, by treasuring up in our minds the most important truths. If we rush into the divine presence with a vacant or ignorant or unprepared mind, with a heart full of the world—as we shall feel no disposition or qualification for the work we are about to engage in—so we cannot expect that our petitions will be heard or granted. There must be some congruity between the heart and the object, some affinity between the state of our minds and the business in which they are employed, if we would expect success in the work.

We are often deceived both as to the principle and the effect of our prayers. When from some external cause, the heart is glad, the spirits light, the thoughts ready, the tongue voluble, a kind of spontaneous eloquence is the result. With this we are pleased, and this ready flow we are willing to impose on ourselves for piety.

On the other hand, when the mind is dejected, the animal spirits low, the thoughts confused, when apposite words do not readily present themselves, we are apt to accuse our hearts of want of fervor, to lament our weakness, and to mourn that, because we have had no pleasure in praying, our prayers have, therefore, not ascended to the throne of mercy. In both cases we perhaps judge ourselves unfairly. These unready accents, these faltering praises, these ill-expressed petitions, may find more acceptance than the florid talk with which we were so well satisfied; the latter consisted, it may be, of shining thoughts, floating on the fancy, eloquent words dwelling on the lips; the former might be the sighing of a contrite spirit abased by the feeling of its own unworthiness and awed by the perfections of a holy and heart-searching God. The heart is dissatisfied with its own dull and tasteless repetitions which, with all their imperfections, Infinite Goodness may perhaps hear with favor.* We

---

*Of these sort of repetitions, our admirable Church Liturgy has been accused as a fault. But this defect, if it be one, happily accommodates itself to our infirmities. Where is the favored being whose heart accompanies his lips in every sentence? Is there no absence of mind in the petitioner, no wandering of the thought, no inconstancy of the heart, which these repetitions are wisely calculated to correct, to rouse the dead attention, to bring back the strayed affections?

may not only be elated with the fluency but even with the fervency of our prayers. Vanity may grow out of the very act of renouncing it, and we may begin to feel proud at having humbled ourselves so eloquently.

There is, however, a strain and spirit of prayer equally distinct from that facility and copiousness for which we certainly are never the better in the sight of God, and from that constraint and dryness for which we may be never the worse. There is a simple, solid, pious strain of prayer in which the supplicant is so filled and occupied with a sense of his own dependence, and of the importance of the things for which he asks, and so persuaded of the power and grace of God through Christ to give him those things that while he is engaged in it, he does not merely imagine but feels assured that God is nigh to him as a reconciled Father, so that every burden and doubt are taken off from his mind. "He knows," as Saint John expresses it, "that he has the petitions he desired of God," and feels the truth of that promise, "while they are yet speaking I will hear." This is the perfection of prayer.

Chapter IV

On the Effects of Prayer

It is objected by a certain class, and on the specious ground of humility too, though we do not always find the objector himself quite as humble as his plea would be thought, that it is arrogant in such insignificant beings as we are to presume to lay our petty necessities before the Great and Glorious God, who cannot be expected to condescend to the multitude of trifling and even interfering requests which are brought before Him by His creatures. These and such like objections arise from mean and unworthy thoughts of the Great Governor of the Universe. It seems as if those who make them considered the Most High as "such a one as themselves": a being who can perform a certain given quantity of business, but who would be overpowered with an additional quantity. Or at best, is it not considering the Almighty in the light not of an Infinite God, but of a great man, of a minister, or a king who, while he superintends public and national concerns, is obliged to neglect small and individual petitions; because his hands being full, he cannot spare that leisure and attention which suffice for everything? They do not consider Him as that infinitely gracious Being who, while He beholds at once all that is doing in heaven and in earth, is at the same time as attentive to the prayer of the poor destitute, as present to the sorrowful sighing of the prisoner, as if each of these forlorn creatures were individually the object of His undivided attention.

These critics, who are for sparing the Supreme Being the

trouble of our prayers, and who, if I may so speak without profaneness, would relieve Omnipotence of part of His burden by assigning to His care only such a portion as may be more easily managed, seem to have no adequate conception of His attributes.

They forget that infinite wisdom puts Him as easily within reach of all knowledge as infinite power does of all performance; that He is a Being in whose plans complexity makes no difficulty, variety no obstruction, and multiplicity no confusion; that to ubiquity distance does not exist; that to infinity space is annihilated; that past, present, and future are discerned more accurately at one glance of His eye, to whom a thousand years are as one day, than a single moment of time or a single point of space can be by ours.

Another class continue to bring forward, as pertinaciously as if it had never been answered, the exhausted argument that seeing God is immutable, no petitions of ours can ever change Him; that events themselves being settled in a fixed and unalterable course, and bound in a fatal necessity, it is folly to think that we can disturb the established laws of the universe or interrupt the course of Providence by our prayers; and that it is absurd to suppose these firm decrees can be reversed by any requests of ours.

Without entering into the wide and trackless field of fate and free will, we would only observe that these objections apply equally to all human actions as well as to prayer. It may therefore with the same propriety be urged that seeing God is immutable and His decrees unalterable, therefore our *actions* can produce no change in Him or in our own state. Weak as well as impious reasoning! It may be questioned whether even the modern French and German philosophers might not be prevailed upon to acknowledge the existence of God if they might make such a use of His attributes.

How much more wisdom as well as happiness results from a humble Christian spirit! Such a plain practical text as "Draw near unto God, and He will draw near unto you" carries more consolation, more true knowledge of his wants and their remedy to the heart of a penitent sinner than all the tomes of casuistry which have puzzled the world ever since the question was first set afloat by its original propounders.

And as the plain man only got up and walked to prove there was such a thing as motion in answer to the philosopher who, in an elaborate theory, denied it; so the plain Christian, when he is borne down with the assurance that there is no efficacy in prayer, requires no better argument to repel the assertion than the good he finds in prayer itself. A Christian knows, because he feels, that prayer is, though in a way to him inscrutable, the medium of connection between God and His rational creatures, the method appointed by Him to draw down His blessings upon us. The Christian knows that prayer is the appointed means of uniting two ideas, one of the highest magnificence, the other of the most profound lowliness, within the compass of the imagination; namely, that it is the link of communication between "the High and Lofty One who inhabiteth eternity" and that heart of the "contrite in which He delights to dwell." He knows that this inexplicable union between beings so unspeakably, so essentially different, can only be maintained by prayer; that this is the strong but secret chain which unites time with eternity, earth with heaven, man with God.

The plain Christian, as was before observed, cannot explain why it is so, but while he *feels* the efficacy, he is contented to let the learned *define* it, and he will no more postpone prayer till he can produce a chain of reasoning on the manner in which he derives benefit from it, than he will postpone eating till he can give a scientific lecture on the nature of digestion. He is contented with knowing that his meat has nourished him, and he leaves to the philosopher, who may choose to defer his meal till he has elaborated his treatise, to starve in the interim. The Christian *feels* better than he is able to explain that the functions of his spiritual life can no more be carried on without habitual prayer than those of his natural life without frequent bodily nourishment. He feels renovation and strength grow out of the use of the appointed means as necessarily in the one case as in the other. He feels that the health of his soul can no more be sustained and its powers kept in continual vigor by the *prayers* of a distant day than his body by the *aliment* of a distant day.

But there is one motive to the duty in question far more constraining to the true believer than all others that can be named, more imperative than any argument on its utility, than any conviction of its efficacy, even than any experience of its consolations. *Prayer is the command of God*, the plain, positive, repeated injunction of the Most High, who declares, "He will be inquired of." This is enough to secure the obedience of the Christian, even though a promise were not, as it always is, attached to the command. But in this case, to our unspeakable comfort, the promise is as clear as the precept *"Ask, and ye shall receive."* This is encouragement enough for the plain Christian. As to the *manner* in which prayer is made to coincide with the general scheme of God's plan in the government of human affairs, how God has left Himself at liberty to reconcile our prayer with His own predetermined will, the Christian does not very critically examine, his precise and immediate duty being to pray and not to examine.

In the mean time it is enough for the humble believer to be assured that the Judge of all the earth is doing right. It is enough for him to be assured in that Word of God "which cannot lie," of numberless actual instances of the efficacy of prayer in obtaining blessings and averting calamities, both national and individual. It is enough for him to be convinced experimentally by that internal evidence, which is perhaps paramount to all other evidence, the comfort he himself has received from prayer, when all other comforts have failed and above all to end with the same motive with which we began, the only motive indeed which *he* requires for the performance of any duty. It is motive enough for him that *Thus saith the Lord.*

Others there are who, perhaps not controverting any of these premises, yet neglect to build practical consequences on the admission of them; who neither denying the duty nor the efficacy of prayer, yet go on to live either in the irregular observance or the total neglect of it, as appetite or pleasure or business or humor may happen to predominate; and who by living almost without prayer, may be said, "to live almost without God in the world." To such we can only say that they little know what they lose. The time is hastening on when they will look upon those blessings as invaluable, which now they think not worth asking for; when they will bitterly regret the absence of those means and opportunities which now they either neglect or despise. "O that they were wise! that they understood this! that they would consider their latter end!"

There are again others who it is to be feared, having once lived in the habit of prayer, yet not having been well grounded in those principles of faith and repentance on which genuine prayer is built, have by degrees totally discontinued it. "They do not find," say they, "that their affairs prosper the better or are the worse; or perhaps they were unsuccessful in their affairs even before they dropped the practice and so have no encouragement to go on." They do not *know* that they had no encouragement; they do not *know* how much worse their affairs might have gone on had they discontinued it sooner, or how their prayers helped to retard their ruin. Or they do not *know* that perhaps "they asked amiss," or that, if they had obtained what they asked, they might have been far more unhappy. For a true believer never "restrains prayer" because he is not certain that he obtains every individual request; for he is persuaded that God, in compassion to our ignorance, sometimes in great mercy withholds what we desire, and often disappoints His most favored children by giving them not what they ask, but what He knows is really good for them. The favored child, as a pious prelate* observes, cries for the shining blade, which the tender parent withholds, knowing it would cut his fingers.

Thus to persevere when we have not the encouragement of visible success is an evidence of tried faith. Of this holy perseverance Job was a noble instance. Defeat and disap-

---

*Bishop Hall

pointment rather stimulated than stopped *his* prayers. Though in a vehement strain of passionate eloquence he exclaims, "I cry out of wrong, but I am not heard: I cry aloud, but there is no judgment," yet so persuaded was he notwithstanding of the duty of continuing this holy importunity, that he persisted against all human hope till he attained to that exalted pitch of unshaken faith by which he was enabled to break out into that sublime apostrophe, "Though He slay me, yet I will trust in Him."

But may we not say that there is a considerable class who not only bring none of the objections which we have stated against the use of prayer; who are so far from rejecting that they are exact and regular in the performance of it; who yet take it up on as low ground as is consistent with their ideas of their own safety; who, while they consider prayer as an indispensable form, believe nothing of that change of heart and of those holy tempers which it is intended to produce? Many, who yet adhere scrupulously to the letter, are so far from entering into the spirit of this duty that they are strongly inclined to suspect those of hypocrisy or fanaticism who adopt the true scriptural views of prayer. Nay, as even the Bible may be so wrested as to be made to speak almost any language in support of almost any opinion, these persons lay hold on Scripture itself to bear them out in their own slight views of this duty; and they profess to borrow from thence the ground of that censure which they cast on the more serious Christians. Among the many passages which have been made to convey a meaning foreign to their original designs, none have been seized upon with more avidity by such persons than the pointed censures of our Savior on those "who for a *pretense* make long prayers," as well as on those "who use vain repetitions, and think they shall be heard for much speaking." Now the things here intended to be reproved were the hypocrisy of the Pharisees and the ignorance of the heathen, together with the error of all those who depended on the success of their prayers, while they imitated the deceit of the one or the folly of the other. But our Savior never meant that those severe reprehensions should cool or abridge the devotion of pious Christians, to which they do not at all apply.

More or fewer words, however, so little constitute the true value of prayer that there is no doubt but one of the most affecting specimens on record is the short petition of the Publican, full fraught as it is with that spirit of contrition and self-abasement which is the very principle and soul of prayer. And this specimen, perhaps, is the best model for that sudden lifting up of the heart which we call ejaculation. But we doubt, in general, whether the few hasty words to which these frugal petitioners would stint the scanty devotions of others and themselves will be always found ample enough to satisfy the humble penitent who, being a sinner has much to confess, who, hoping he is a pardoned sinner has much to acknowledge. Such a one, perhaps, cannot always pour out the fullness of his soul within the prescribed abridgments.

Even the sincerest Christian, when he wishes to find his heart warm, has often to lament its coldness though he feels that he has received much and has therefore much to be thankful for, yet he is not able at once to bring his wayward spirit into such a posture as shall fit it for the solemn duty. Such a one has not merely his form to repeat, but he has his tempers to reduce to order, his affections to excite, and his peace to make. His thoughts may be realizing the sarcasm of the Prophet on the idol Baal, "they may be gone on a journey" and must be recalled; his heart, perhaps, "sleepeth and must be awaked." A devout supplicant too will labor to affect and warm his mind with a sense of the great and gracious attributes of God, in imitation of the holy men of old. Like Jehoshaphat, he will sometimes enumerate "the power and the might, and the mercies of the Most High" in order to stir up the sentiments of awe and gratitude and love and humility in his own soul.* He will labor to imitate the example of his Savior, whose heart dilated with the expression of the same holy affections: "I thank thee, O Father, Lord of heaven and earth." A heart thus animated, thus warmed with divine love, cannot always scrupulously

*2 Chron. 20:5–6.

limit itself to the mere *business* of prayer, if I may so speak. It cannot content itself with merely spreading out its own necessities, but expands in contemplating the perfections of Him to whom he is addressing them.

The humble supplicant, though he be no longer *governed* by a love of the world, yet grieves to find that he cannot totally exclude it from his thoughts. Though he has on the whole a deep sense of his own wants and of the abundant provision which is made for them in the Gospel, yet, when he most wishes to be rejoicing in those strong motives for love and gratitude, alas, even then he has to mourn his worldliness, his insensibility, his deadness. He has to deplore the littleness and vanity of the objects which are even then drawing away his heart from his Redeemer. The best Christian is but too liable, during the temptations of the day, to be ensnared by "the lust of the eye, and the pride of life," and is not always brought without effort to reflect that he is but dust and ashes. How can even good persons, who are just come, perhaps, from listening to the flattery of their fellow worms, acknowledge before God, without any preparation of the heart, that they are miserable sinners? They require a little time to impress on their own souls the truth of that solemn confession of sin which they are making to Him, without which brevity and not length might constitute hypocrisy.

Even the sincerely pious have in prayer grievous wanderings to lament, from which others mistakenly suppose the advanced Christian to be exempt. Such wanderings that, as an old divine has observed, it would exceedingly humble a good man, could he, after he had prayed, be made to see his prayers written down, with exact interlineations of all the vain and impertinent thoughts which had thrust themselves in amongst them. So that such a one will, indeed, from a strong sense of these distractions, feel deep occasion, with the Prophet, to ask forgiveness for the "iniquity of his *holy* things," and would find cause enough for humiliation every night, had he to lament the sins of his prayers only.

We know that such a brief petition as "Lord help my unbelief," if the supplicant be in so happy a frame, and the prayer be darted up with such strong faith that his very soul mounts with the petition, may suffice to draw down a blessing which may be withheld from the more prolix petitioner. Yet if by prayer we do not mean a mere form of words, whether it be long or short, but that secret communion between God and the soul which is the very breath and being of religion, then is the Scripture so far from suggesting that short measure of which it is accused, that it expressly says, "Pray without ceasing"; "Pray evermore"; "I will that men pray everywhere"; "Continue instant in prayer."

If such "repetitions," as these objectors reprobate, stir up desires as yet unawakened or protract affections already excited (for "*vain* repetitions" are such as awaken or express no new desire and serve no religious purpose), then are "repetitions" not to be condemned. And that our Savior did not give the warning against "long prayers and repetitions" in the sense these objectors allege is evident from His own practice, for once we are told "He continued *all night* in prayer to God." And again, in a most awful crisis of His life, it is expressly said, "He prayed the *third* time, using *the same words.*"

All habits gain by exercise. Of course the Christian graces gain force and vigor by being called out and, as it were, mustered in prayer. Love, faith, and trust in the divine promises, if they were not kept alive by this stated intercourse with God, would wither and die.

Chapter V

Vain Excuses for the Neglect of Prayer

There are not a few who offer apologies for the neglect of spiritual duties by saying they believe them to be right, but that they are tempted to neglect the exercise of them by idleness or business, by company or pleasure. This may be true, but temptations are not compulsions. The great adversary of souls may fill the fancy with alluring images of enjoyment, so as to draw us away from any duty, but it is in our own choice either to indulge or through grace to repel them. He may act upon the passion through outward objects which introduce them to the mind through the senses, but the grace of God enables all who faithfully ask it to withstand them.

If we were not at liberty to reject temptation, sin would be no sin. It is the offer of the grace of resistance not used which makes the offender to be without excuse. All the motives and the allurements to sin would be ineffectual, would we keep up in our minds what are its "wages": death. Death spiritual, death eternal!

Of all the excuses for the neglect of prayer, the man of business justifies his omission to himself by the most plausible apologies. Many of this class, active for themselves and useful to the world, are far from disputing either the propriety or the duty of prayer; they are willing, however, for the present, to turn over this duty to the clergy, to the idle, to women and children. They allow it to be an important thing, but not the most important. They acknowledge, if men have time to spare, they cannot spend it better, but *they* have no time. It is indeed a duty, but a duty not to be compared with that of the court, the bar, the public office, the counting-house, or the shop.

Now, in pleading for the importance of the one, we should be the last to detract from that of the other. We only plead for their entire compatibility.

We pass over the instance of Daniel, a man of business and a statesman, and of many other public characters recorded in Scriptures, and confine ourselves to the example of Nehemiah. He was not only an officer in the court of the greatest king of the East, but it was his duty to be much in the royal presence. He was, on a particular occasion, under deep affliction; for Jerusalem was in ruins! On a certain day his madness was so great as to be visible to the king, at whose table he was attending.

The monarch enquired the cause of his sorrow and what request he had to make. He instantly "prayed to the God of heaven," doubtless to strengthen him, and then made his position to the king for no less a boon than to allow him to rebuild the walls of the sacred city. His prayer preceded his position. It was that prayer which gave him courage to present that petition and which probably induced the sovereign to grant it. What a double encouragement is here given to the courtier both to pray to God and to speak truth to a king!

Though the plea of the man of business for his own particular exemption can by no means be granted, yet it is the sense he entertains of the value of his professional duties, which deceives him. It leads him to believe that there can be no evil in substituting business for devotion. He is conscious that he is industrious, and he knows that industry is a great moral quality. He is rightly persuaded that the man of pleasure has no such plea to produce. He therefore imposes on himself, with the belief that there can be no harm in substituting a moral for a religious exercise; for he has learned to think highly of morality, while he assigns to religion only an inferior degree on his scale of duties.

He usually goes to church once on the Sunday, but it does not at all infringe on his religious system to examine his accounts, to give a great dinner, or to begin a journey on that day.

Now it is a serious truth that there is no man to whom prayer is more imperatively a duty, or more obviously a necessity, than to the man of business, whether in the higher or the middle classes of society. There is no man who more stands in need of quieting his anxieties, regulating his tempers, cooling his spirits by a devout application for the blessing of God; none to whom it is more necessary to implore the divine protection for the duties or preservation from the dangers of the scene in which he is about to engage; none to whom it is more important to solicit direction in the difficulties which the day may produce; none on whom it is more incumbent to solicit support against the temptations which may be about to assail him; none to whom the petition for an enlightened conscience, an upright intention, a sound probity, and an undeviating sincerity, is of more importance.

What is so likely as prayer to enable him to stand prepared to meet the accidental fluctuations in his affairs, to receive without inebriation a sudden flow of prosperous fortune, or to sustain any adverse circumstances with resignation?

Even persons in more retired situations, even those who have made considerable advances in religion, cannot but acknowledge how much the ordinary and necessary cares of daily life, especially, how much any unexpected accession to them, are likely to cause absence and distraction in their devotions. How much then ought they, whose whole life is business, to be on their guard against these dangers, to double their vigilance against them, and to implore direction under them.

Were the Christian militant accustomed never to engage in the moral battle of daily life without putting on this panoply, the shafts of temptation would strike with a feeble and erring blow; they would not so deeply pierce the guarded heart. And were fervent humble daily prayer once conscientiously adopted, its effects would reach beyond the weekday engagements. It would gradually extend its benign influence to the postponing of settling accounts, the festive dinner, and the not absolutely necessary journey, to one of those six days in which we are enjoined to labor. It would lead him to the habit of doing "no manner of work" on that day, in which the doing of it was prohibited by the great Lawgiver in His own person.

We have more than once alluded to the diversities of character, occasional events, difference in the state of mind as well as of circumstances, which may not only render the prayer which is suitable to one man unsuitable to another, but suitable to the same man under every alteration of circumstances.

But among the proper topics for prayer, there is one, which being of universal interest, ought not to be omitted. For by whatever dissimilarity of character, capacity, profession, station, or temper, the condition of man and, of course, the nature of prayer is diversified, there is one grand point of union, one circumstance, one condition, in which they must all meet; one state, of which every man is equally certain; one event which happeneth to all: "It is appointed unto every man once to die." The rugged road of sorrow, the flowery path of pleasure, as well as

The paths of glory, lead but to the grave.

In praying, therefore, against the fear of death, we do not pray against a contingent but a certain evil. We pray to be delivered from the overwhelming dread of that house which is appointed for all living. We are put in mind that all who are born must die!

"The end of all things is at hand." To what purpose does the apostle convert this awful proclamation? Does he use it to encourage gloomy tempers, to invite to unprofitable melancholy? No. He uses the solemn admonition to stir us up to more goodness. Therefore, "be sober." He does more. He uses it to excite us to religious vigilance "and watch unto prayer."

Prayer against the fear of death, by keeping up in us a constant remembrance of our mortality, will help to wean us from a too intimate attachment to the things we are so soon to quit. By this habitual preparation to meet our Judge, we shall be brought to pray more earnestly for an interest in the great Intercessor, and to arrive more effectually against every offense which may aggravate the awfulness of that meeting.

Fervent prayer, that divine grace may prepare us for death, will, if cordially adopted, answer many great moral purposes. It will remind every individual of every class that "the time is short," that "there is no repentance in the grave."

Perhaps even the worldly and thoughtless man, under an occasional fit of dejection or an accidental disappointment, may be brought to say, "When I am in heaviness, I will think upon God." Oh, think upon Him, call upon Him *now*—now, when you are in prosperity; now, when your fortunes are flourishing; now, when your hill is so strong that you think it shall never be removed. Think upon Him, call upon Him when the scene is the brightest, when the world courts, flatteries invite, and pleasures betray you. Think on Him while you are able to think at all, while you possess the capacity of thinking. The time may come when "He may turn His face from you, and you will be troubled." Think of God when the alluring images of pleasure and of profit would seduce you from Him. Prosperity is the season of peculiar peril. "It is the bright day that brings forth the adder." Think of God when the tempting world says, "All this I will give thee." Trust not the insolvent world, it has cheated every creditor that ever trusted it. It will cheat you.

To the *man of opulence*, who heaps up riches and cannot tell who shall gather them, prayer will be a constant memento. It will remind him that he walks in a vain shadow and disquiets himself in vain. It will remind him of laying up treasures where thieves cannot enter, nor rust corrode.

The habit of praying against the fear of death would check the pride of youthful *beauty* by reminding her how soon it must say to the worm, "Thou art my father," and to corruption, "Thou art my mother and sister."

To the *man of genius*, he who thought that of making

many books there would be no end; who, in his zeal to write, had neglected to pray; who thought little of any immortality but that which was to be conferred by the applause of dying creatures like himself; who, in the vanity of possessing talents, had forgotten that he must one day account for the application of them; if happily he should be brought to see the evil of his own heart, to feel the wants of his own soul, how intense will be his repentance, how deep his remorse that he had loved the praise of men more than the praise of God! How fervently will he pray that his mercies may not aggravate the account of his sins, that his talents may not become the instrument of his punishment! How earnestly will he supplicate for pardon, how devoutly will he "give glory to God, before his feet stumbles on the dark mountains"!

The *man of business*, to whom we have already adverted, who thought his schemes so deeply laid, his speculations so prudently planned, that nothing could frustrate them; who calculated that the future was as much in his power as the present, forgot that death, that grand subverter of projects, might interpose his *veto*—this man, who could not find time to pray, must find time to die. He may at length find (happy if he ever had it) that he cannot meet his end with a peaceful heart and a resigned spirit without the preparation of prayer for support in that awful period, "when his purposes shall be broken off and all his thoughts perish."

The *man of pleasure*—alas! what shall we say for him? He is sunk to the lowest step of degradation in the moral scale. He has not even human supports. He has robbed himself even of the ordinary consolations resorted to by ordinary men. He has no stay on which to lay hold, no twig at which to catch, no pretense by which to flatter himself into a false peace, no recollection of past usefulness. He has neither served his country nor benefited society. What shall we say for him? If he pray not for himself, we must pray for him—with God all things are possible.

The *statesman*, indefatigable in the public service, distinguished for integrity, but neglecting the offices of Christianity; whose lofty character power had not warped, nor cupidity debased; but whose religious principles, though they had never been renounced, had not been kept in exercise; a spirit of rare disinterestedness; a moralist of unblanched honor, but who pleaded that duty had left him little time for devotion! Should divine grace incline him at last to seek God, should he begin to pray to be prepared for death and judgment, he will deeply regret with the contrite cardinal, not that he served his king faithfully, but that his higher services had not been devoted to their highest object. In this frame of mind, that ambition which was satisfied with what earth could give or kings reward, will appear no longer glorious in his eyes. True and just to his sovereign, devoted to his country, faithful to all but his Savior and himself, he now laments that he had neglected to seek a better country; neglected to serve the King Eternal, the blessed and only Potentate; neglected to obtain an interest in a kingdom which shall not be moved. He feels that mere patriotism, grand as is its object, and important as is its end, will not afford support to a soul sinking at the approach of the inevitable hour, awed at the view of final judgment.

But these great and honorable persons are the very men to whom superior cares and loftier duties and higher responsibilities render prayer even more necessary, were it possible, than to others. Nor does this duty trench upon other duties, for the compatibility of prayer is universal. It is an exercise which has the property of incorporating itself with every other; not only not impending, but adventing it. If secular thoughts and vain imaginations often break in on our devout employments, let us allow Religion to vindicate her rights by uniting herself with our worldly occupations. There is no crevice so small at which devotion may not slip in; in no other instance of so rich a blessing being annexed to so easy a condition; no other case in which there is any certainty, that to ask is to have. This the suitors to the great do not always find so easy from them as the great themselves may find from God.

Not only the elevation on which they stand makes this fence necessary for their personal security, by enabling them to bear the height without giddiness, but the guidance of God's hand is so essential to the operations they conduct, that the public prosperity, no less than their own safety, is involved in the practice of habitual prayer. God will be more likely to bless the hand which steers and the head which directs when both are ruled by the heart which prays. Happily we need not look out of our own age or nation for instances of public men who, while they govern the country, are themselves governed by a religious principle, who petition the Almighty for direction, and praise Him for success.

The *hero* who, in the hot engagement, surrounded with the "pride, pomp, and circumstance of war," bravely defied death, forgot all that was personal and only remembered—nobly remembered—his country and his immediate duty, animated with the glory that was to be acquired with his arm and almost ready to exclaim with the Roman patriot:

—What pity
That we can die but once to serve our country!

Yet this hero, if he had ever made a conscience of prayer, may he not hereafter find that the most successful instrumentality is a distinct thing in itself and will be different in its results from personal piety? May he not find that, though he saved others, himself he cannot save?

If, however, in later life, in the cool shade of honorable retirement, he be brought through the grace of God to habituate himself to earnest prayer, he will deeply regret that he ever entered the field of battle without imploring the favor of the God of battles, that he had ever returned alive from slaughtered squadrons, without adoring the Author of his providential preservation. If his penitence be sincere, his prayer will be effectual. It will fortify him under the more depressing prospect of that death which is soon to be encountered in the solitude of his darkened chamber; without witnesses, without glory; without the cheering band; without the spirit-stirring drum; without the tumultuous acclamation; with no objects to distract his attention; no conflicting concerns to divide his thoughts; no human arms, either of others or his own, on which to depend. This timely reflection—this late, though never *too* late prayer—may still prepare him for a peaceful dying-bed; may lead him to lean on a stronger arm than his own or that of an army; may conduct him to a victory over his last enemy and thus dispose him to meet death in a safer state than when he despised it in the field; may bring him to acknowledge that while he continued to live without subjection to the Captain of his salvation, though he had fought bravely, he had not yet fought the good fight.

Chapter VI

Characters Who Reject Prayer

Among the many articles of erroneous calculation, to which so much of the sin and misery of life may be attributed, the neglect or misuse of prayer will not form the lightest. The prophet Jeremiah, in his impassioned address to the Almighty, makes no distinction between those who acknowledge no God and those who live without prayer: "Pour out Thy fury, O Lord, upon the heathen, and upon the families that call not upon Thy name."*

Some duties are more incumbent on some persons, and some on others; depending on the difference of talents, wealth, leisure, learning, station, and opportunities; but the duty of prayer is of imperative obligation. It is universal because it demands none of any of the above requisites. It demands only a willing heart, a consciousness of sin, a sense of dependence, a feeling of helplessness. Those who voluntarily neglect it shut themselves out from the presence of their Maker. "I know you not," must assuredly be the sentence of exclusion on those who thus "know not God."

---

*We have not thought it necessary to touch upon family or public worship, assuming that those who habitually observe private prayer will conscientiously attend to the more public exercises of devotion; and when it is recollected that the divine Being, who performed a miracle to feed the multitude, that He might set an example of prayer in every possible form, previously blessed the simple but abundant meal, how shall a *dependent* creature dare omit a duty sanctified.

Nothing, it is true, can exclude them from His inspection, but they exclude themselves from His favor.

Many nearly renounce prayer by affecting to make it so indefinite a thing as not to require regular exercise. Just as many also unhallow the Sabbath, who pretend they do nothing on weekdays which they should fear to do on Sundays. The truth is, instead of sanctifying the weekdays by raising them to the duties of Sunday (which is indeed impracticable, let men talk as they please), they desecrate the Sabbath to secular purposes, and so contrive to keep no Sunday at all.

Stated seasons for indispensable employments are absolutely necessary for so desultory, so versatile a creature as man. That which is turned over to any chance time is seldom done at all, and those who despise the recurrence of appointed times and seasons are only less censurable than those who rest in them.

Other duties and engagements have their allotted seasons. Why, then, should the most important duty in which an immortal being can be employed, by being left to accident, become liable to occasional omission, liable to increasing neglect, liable to total oblivion?

All the other various works of God know their appointed times: the seasons, the heavenly bodies, day and night, seed-time and harvest. All set an example of undeviating regularity. Why should man, the only thinking being, be the only disorderly work of Almighty power?

But while we are asserting the necessity of seasons of prayer, let us not be suspected of attaching undue importance to them; for all these are but the framework, the scaffolding, the mere mechanical and subsidiary adjuncts. They are but the preparations for Christian worship. They remind us, they intimate to us, that an important work is to be done, but are no part of the work itself.

They, therefore, who most insist on the value of stated devotions, must never lose sight of that grand and universal prime truth, that wherever we are, still we are in God's presence; whatever we have is His gift; whatever we hope is His promise; feelings which are commensurate with all times, all places, and limited to no particular scenes or seasons.

There is in some, in many it is to be feared, a readiness to acknowledge this general doctrine, which what is miscalled natural religion teaches, but who are far from including in their system the peculiarities, the duties, the devotions of Christianity. These are decorous men of the world, who, assuming the character of philosophical liberality, value themselves on having shaken off the shackles of prejudice, superstition, and system. They acknowledge a Creator of the universe, but it is in a vague and general way. They worship a Being "whose temple is all space," that is, everywhere but in the human heart. They put Him as far as possible from themselves. Believing He has no providential care of them, they feel no personal interest in Him. God and nature are with them synonymous terms. That the creation of the world was His work, they do not go the length of denying; but that its government is in His hands is with them very problematical.

In any case, however, they are assured that a Being of such immensity requires not the littleness of superstitious forms, nor the petty limitations of stated seasons and regular devotions; that He is infinitely above attending to our paltry concerns, though God Himself anticipated this objection when He condescended to declare, "He that offereth Me thanks and praise, he honoreth Me."

One says, *he* can adore the Author of nature in the contemplation of His works; that the mountains and the fields are *His* altar for worship. Another says that his notion of religion is to deal honestly in his commerce with the world; both insist that they can serve God anywhere and everywhere. We know they can and we hope they do. But our Savior, who knew the whole make of man, his levity, instability, and unfixedness, and who was yet no friend to the formalist or the superstitious, not only commands, at the hour of prayer, our entering into the closet, but our shutting the door—a tacit reproof, perhaps, of the devotion of the Saddocean, as well as the publicity of the Pharisaic religion, but certainly an admonition of general obligation.

In treating of prayer, it would be a superfluous labor to address unbelievers with the same arguments or persuasions which we would humbly propose to such as aver, with whatever degree of conviction, their belief in Christianity. It would be folly to address them with motives drawn from a book which they do not believe or do not read. With those who are ignorant of the first principles of religion, or those who reject them, we have no common ground on which to stand. Saint Paul, with his usual discrimination has left us an example in this as well as in all other cases. With the philosophical Athenians, he confined his reasonings to natural religion. To the Jewish king Agrippa, who "believed the prophets," in telling the story of his own conversion, he most judiciously introduced the great doctrines of remission of sins and justification by faith.

If the Pyrrhonist in question were to see a genuine Christian character delineated in all its dimensions, marked with its fair lineaments, and enlivened by its quickening spirit, such, for instance, as is exemplified in the character of Saint Paul, he would consider it as a mere picture of the imagination, and would no more believe its reality than he believes that of Xenophon's Prince, the Stoic's Wise Man, Quintillian's Perfect Orator, or any other Platonic or Utopian representation. Or could he be brought to believe its actual existence, he would set such a man far above the necessity of prayer; he would emancipate him in his own independent worth. For how should he ever suspect that such a man would ever pray at all, much less would be in prayer more abundant, in humiliation more profound, in self-renunciation more abased?

Is it not probable that some of those inquiring minds, who adorned the Porch and the Academy, as well as the more favored men under the old dispensation, who saw the future through the dim and distant perspective of prophecy, would have rejoiced to see the things which you see and have not believed?

How gratefully would many of these illustrious spirits have accepted advantages which you overlook! How joyfully would they have received from Him who cannot lie the assurance that if they would seek of Him that truth after which they "were feeling," they should find it! How gladly would that sublime and elegant spirit, whose favorite theme was pure spiritual love, have listened to the great apostle of love; to him who caught the flame as he leaned on the bosom of his affectionate Master!

How would this same exalted genius, who taught the immortality of the soul to the bright yet blind Athenians—he, whose penetrating mind rather guessed than knew what he taught; whose keen eye caught some glimpse of a brighter state through the darkness which surrounded him—how would he have gloried in that light and immortality which the Gospel revelation has brought to light? But with what unspeakable rapture would he have learned that He who revealed the life could give it, that He who promised immortality could *bestow* it! With what obedient transport would he have heard this touching apostrophe, at once a strong reproof and a tender invitation: "Ye will not come unto me that ye might have life!" Ye philosophizing cavilers, who live in the meridian splendor of this broad day, "how will *you* escape, if you neglect so great salvation"?

But if pride, the dominant intellectual sin, keeps the skeptic aloof from the humiliating duties of devotion, the habitual indulgence of the senses, in another class, proves an equal cause of alienating the heart from prayer.

The man absorbed by ease and enjoyment, and sunk in the relaxing softness of a voluptuous life, has a natural distaste to everything that stands in opposition to the delights of that life. It is the smoothness of his course which makes it so slippery. He is lost before he feels that he is sinking. For whether we plunge at once from a precipitous height or slide down from it on an inclined plane, still, while there is a yawning gulf at the bottom, our destruction is equally inevitable.

The systematic but decorous sensualist is one whose life is a course of sober luxury, of measured indulgence. He contrives to reconcile an abandonment of sound principle with a kind of orderly practice. He inquires rather what is decent than what is right; what will secure the favorable opinion of the world, especially his own class, rather than what will please God. His object is to make the most of this world. Selfishness has established his throne in his heart. His study is to make every thing and every person subservient to his convenience or pleasure or profit, yet without glaringly trespassing on the laws of propriety or custom. Self is the source and center of all his actions. But though this governing principle is always on the watch for its gratification, yet as part of that gratification depends on a certain degree of reputation, it frequently leads him to do right things, though without right motives, for the mainspring sometimes sets the right in motion as well as the wrong.

He goes to church on all public occasions, but without devotion; gives alms without charity; subscribes to public institutions without being interested in their prosperity, except as they are frequently succeeded by a pleasant dinner and good company, and as the subscription list of names he knows will be published. He lives on good terms with different and even opposite classes of men without being attached to any. He does them favors with affectation, knowing that he shall have occasion to solicit favors in return, for he never does a small kindness without a view to asking a greater.

He deprecates excess in everything but always lives upon its confines.

Prayer enters not into his plan. He has nothing to ask, for he has all in himself. Thanksgiving is still less his practice, for what he has he deserves.

He had read that "to enjoy is to obey," and he is always ready to give you this cheerful proof of the most unlimited obedience. He respects the laws of the country, especially such as guard property and game, and eagerly punishes the violators of both. But as to the laws of God, he thinks they were made to guard the possessions of the rich, to punish the vicious poor, and to frighten those who have nothing to lose. Yet he respects some of the commandments and would placard on every post and pillar that which says, "Thou shalt not steal," while he thinks that which says, "Thou shalt not covet," might be expunged from the Decalogue.

If you happen to speak of the helplessness of man, he thinks you are alluding to some paralytic; if of his dependence, to some hanger-on of a great man; if of his sinfulness, he adopts your opinion, for he reads the Newgate Calendar. But of sin, as an inherent principle, of the turpitude of sin, except as it disturbs society, he knows nothing. But religion as a principle of action, but prayer as a source of peace or a ground of hope, he neither knows nor desires to know. The stream of life glides smoothly on without it. Why should he ruffle its placid flow! Why should he break in on the course of enjoyment with self-imposed austerities? He believes himself to be respected by his fellow men, and the favor of God is not in all his thoughts. His real character the great day of decisions will discover. Till then he will have two characters.

"Soul, take thine ease, thou hast much goods laid up for thee," is perhaps the state of all others which most disqualifies and unfits for prayer. Not only the apostrophe excites the bodily appetite, but the *soul* is called upon to contemplate, to repose on the soothing prospect, the delights of that voluptuousness for which the "much goods are laid up."

But when the prosperous fool says, "Soul, take thine ease; thou hast much goods laid up for thee," the prosperous Christian says, "Soul, tremble at thine ease; be on thy guard. Thou hast, indeed, much goods laid up for thee, but it is in a future world. Lose not a large inheritance for a paltry possession. Forfeit not an unalienable reversion for a life interest, a life which this very night may be required of thee."

Thus we see what restrains prayer in these two classes of character. The skeptic does not pray, because he does not believe that God is a hearer of prayer; the voluptuary, because he believes that God is such a one as himself, and because he has already gotten all that he wants of Him. His gold, and the means of gratifying his sensuality, would not be augmented by the dry duties of devotion, and with an exercise which would increase neither, he can easily dispense.

Chapter VII

Errors in Prayer

It has lately been observed by a distinguished Christian orator that "many profess to believe the Bible to be true, who do not believe the truths *in* the Bible." So may we not say that all desire the gifts of God, but they do not desire God. If we profess to love Him, it is for our own sake. When shall we begin to love Him for Himself? Many who do not go the length of omitting prayer, but pray merely from custom or education, frequently complain that they find no benefit from prayer; others that they experience not the support and comfort promised to it. May not those who thus complain and who perhaps are far from being enemies to religion find, on a serious examination of their own hearts and lives, some irregularity in desire to be the cause of their discontent and alleged punishment?

We are more disposed to lay down rules for the regulation of God's government than to submit our will to it as He has settled it. If we do not now see the efficacy of the prayer which He has enjoined us to present to Him, it may yet be producing its effect in another way. Infinite wisdom is not obliged to inform us of the manner or the time of His operations. What He expects of us is to persevere in the duty. The very obedience to the command is no small thing whatever be its imperceptible effects.

Under the apparent failure of our prayers, the sources of our repinings must be looked for in the fact of our own blindness and imperfection. For the declarations of the Gospel are sure. Their answer must be found in the grace of

God in Christ Jesus, for His mercies are infallible. Wherever there is disappointment, we may be assured that it is not because He is wanting to us, but because we are wanting to ourselves.

The prophet's expression, "the iniquity of our holy things," will not be thoroughly understood except by those who thus seriously dive into the recesses of their own heart, feel their deficiencies, mark their wanderings, detect and lament their vain imaginations and impertinent thoughts. It is to be regretted that these worldly trifles are far more apt to introduce on us in prayer than the devout affections excited by prayer are to follow us into the world. Business and pleasure break in on our devotions. When will the spirit of devotion mix with the concerns of the world?

You who lament the disappointment of your requests, suffer a few friendly hints. Have you not been impatient because you receive not the things that you asked for immediately? How do you know, but that if you had persevered, God might have bestowed them? He certainly would, had He not in His wisdom foreseen they would not have been good for you and therefore in His mercy withheld them. Is there not some secret, unsuspected infidelity lurking behind such impatience? Is it not virtually saying there is no God to hear or that He is unfaithful to His promise? For is it not absolute impiety to insinuate an accusation that the Supreme Judge of men and angels is capable of injustice or liable to error? God has pleasure in the prosperity of His children. He neither grants nor denies any thing which is not accurately weighed and measured, which is not exactly suited to their wants, if not to their requests.

If we pray aright, it may please God not only to grant that for which we pray, but that for which we do not pray. Supplicating for the best things as we before observed, we may receive inferior and unrequested things, as was the case with Solomon in his prayer for wisdom. God will not forget our labor of love. If He does not seem to notice it at present, He may lay it by for a time when it may be more wanted.

In prayer we must take care not to measure our necessities by our desires; the former are few, the latter may be insatiable. A murmuring spirit is a probable cause why our petitions are not granted. He who murmurs, distrusts the truth of God. And from distrust to infidelity the distance is not great. The certain way to prevent our obtaining what we desire or enjoying what we have is to feel impatient at what we do not receive or to make an improper use of what has been granted to our prayers.

Or you may perhaps address God with sinister and corrupt views, as if you had left His omniscience out of His attributes, as if He might be entrapped with the "secret ambush of a specious prayer." Your design in the application of the boss you solicit may not be for His glory. It may be the prayer of ambition cloaked under the guise of more extensive usefulness. It may be the prayer of covetousness under the pretext of providing for your family. It may be the prayer of injustice, a petition for success in some undertaking for yourself, to the circumvention of another's fairer claim. God, in mercy to our souls, refuses the gift which would endanger them.

Thus, then, if we ask and receive not because we ask deceitfully or blindly, we must not wonder if our prayers are not answered. Or if we obtain what we solicit and turn it to a bad account or to no account at all, we must not be surprised if divine grace is withheld or withdrawn.

The same ill results may be expected if we ask formally or carelessly. Who has not felt that there is a kind of mechanical memory in the tongue which runs over the form without any aid of the understanding, without any concurrence of the will, without any consent of the affections? For do we not sometimes implore God to hear a prayer to which we ourselves are not attending? And is not this presumptuously to demand from Him that attention which we ourselves are not giving to our own requests, even while we are in the act of making them?

A mere superficial form, by lulling the conscience, hardens the heart. The task is performed, but in what manner, or to what result, is not enquired. Genuine prayer is the homage of the soul to God and not an expedient to pacify Him.

If you observe the form but forget the dispositions it is intended to produce, it is evident the end of such prayer is not answered. Yet be not so far discouraged by feeling no sensible effect from prayer as to discontinue it. It is still a right thing to be found in the way of duty.

But perhaps you neglect to implore the Spirit of Christ toward the direction of your prayers and His intercession for their acceptance. As there is no other name through which we can be heard, we must not sever His mediation from His atonement. All His divine offices are not only in perfect harmony, but in inseparable union.* Or perhaps you have used the name of the Redeemer for form's sake or as an accustomed close to your petitions without imploring His efficacious grace in changing your heart as well as in pardoning your sins.

Perhaps you think it is a sufficient qualification for acceptable prayer that you are always forming good intentions; now, though these make up the value of good actions, yet good intentions, not acted upon, when occasion invites and duty calls, will not lessen, but inflame the reckoning. For does it not look as if you had resisted the offer of that Holy Spirit which had originally prompted the intention, and may it not induce Him to withdraw His blessed influence when they have been both invited and rejected?

Do you never, by unwholesome reading, fill the mind with images unfavorable to serious exercise? The children of the pure and holy God should feed on the bread of their Father's house and not on the husks of the prodigal.

Do you never use profanely or lightly that name which is above every name? He who made the ear, shall He not hear? And if He has heard during the day His awful name used by the thoughtless as an expletive or by the impious as an interjection or by the presumptuous as an imprecation, will

---

*We observe with regret that in many public forms of prayer the aid of His mediation is much more frequently implored than the benefits of His death and merits. He is, indeed, our divine Intercessor, but His mere intercession is not the whole source of our dependence on Him.

He in the morning be called on as a Savior and in the evening as an Intercessor?

But it cannot be too frequently repeated that no profession of faith, however orthodox; no avowal of trust in Christ, however confident; no entreaty for the aid of the Spirit, however customary, will avail, if it be not such an influential faith, such a practical trust, such a living devotedness as shall be productive of holiness of heart and life, as shall tend to produce obedience to the commands and submission to the will of God. This is an infallible test by which you may try every doctrine, every principle of the Gospel. We do not mean the truth of them, for that is immutable, but your own actual belief, your own actual interest in them. If no such effects are visible, we deceive ourselves, and the principles we profess are not those by which we are governed.

Prayer is so obviously designed to humble the proud heart of the natural man, by giving him a feeling sense of his misery, his indigence, and his helplessness, that we should be unwilling to believe that even the proudest man can carry his pride to the Throne of Grace except to supplicate deliverance from it. Yet such a character is usually drawn by Him who knew the thoughts and intents of the heart of man, and a long consideration will teach us that the "two men who went up into the temple to pray" were not intended as individual portraits, but as specimens of a class.

The proud man does not, perhaps, always thank God that he is not guilty of adultery or extortion, to which vices he may have little temptation; nor does he glory in paying tithe and taxes, to which the law would compel him. Yet is he never disposed, like the Pharisee, to proclaim the catalog of his own virtues, to bring in his comparative claims, as if it were a good thing to be better than the bad? Is he never disposed to carry in his eye, (as if he would remind his Maker of his superiority), certain persons who are possibly less the objects of divine displeasure than he, by his pride and selfishness, may have rendered himself; although his regularity in the forms of devotion may have made him more respectable in the world, than the poor reprobated being whom he praises God he does not resemble? It is the lowly abasement, the touching self-condemnation, the avowed poverty, the pleaded misery of the destitute beggar that finds acceptance. It is the hungry whom God's mercy fills with good things. It is the rich in his own conceit whom His displeasure sends away empty.

Whenever you are tempted to thank God that you are not like other men, let it be in comparing your own condition with that of the afflicted and bereaved among your own friends. Compare yourself with the paralytic on his couch, with the blind beggar by the wayside, with the laborer in the mine. Think on the wretch in the galleys, on the condemned in the dungeons of despotic governments. Above all, think—and this is the intolerable *acme* of sin in the inflictor and of misery in the sufferer—think on the wretched negro chained in the hold of a slave ship! Think seriously on these and put pride into your prayer if you can. Think on these not to triumph in your own superiority, but to adore the undeserved mercy of God in giving you blessings to which you have no higher claim, and let your praise of yourself be converted into prayer for them.

For there are no dispositions of the heart which are more eminently promoted by prayer than contentment and patience. They are two qualities of the same color, but of different shades, and are generally, when found at all, found in the same breast. Both are the offspring of genuine religion; both nurtured by cordial prayer. The cultivation of the one, under easy circumstances, prepares for the exercise of the other in more trying situations. Both emanate from the same divine principle but are drawn out by different occasions and exercised under varying circumstances.

Content is the tranquility of the heart; prayer is its aliment. It is satisfied under every dispensation of Providence and takes thankfully its allotted portion, never inquiring whether a little more would not be a little better, knowing that if God had so judged, it would have been as easy for Him to have given the more as the less. That is not true content, which does not enjoy as the gift of Infinite

Wisdom what it has, nor is that true patience which does not suffer meekly the loss of what it had because it is not His will that it should have it longer. The language of the patient man under trials is, "It is the Lord." "Shall a living man complain?" is his interrogation. "A good man," says Solomon, "is satisfied from himself." Here the presumptuous might put in *his* claim to the title. But his pretension arises from his mistake, for his satisfaction is *with himself*, that of the Christian with Providence. It arises from the grace of God shed abroad in his heart, which is become a perennial spring of consolation and enjoyment, and which, by persevering prayer, is indented into his very soul. Content knows how to want and how to abound. This is the language of equanimity: "Shall I not receive evil from the hand of the Lord, as well as good?" This is the language of patience. Content is always praising God for what she possesses; patience is always justifying Him for what she suffers. The cultivation of the one effectually prepares us for the exercise of the other. But these dispositions are not inherent in the human heart. How are they generated? By the influence of the Holy Spirit. How are they kept alive? By heartfelt devotion.

Perhaps the impediment which hinders the benefit of prayer in characters apparently correct may be the fatal habit of indulging in some secret sin, the private cherishing of some wrong propensity, the fondly entertaining of some evil imagination. Not being accustomed to control at other times, it intrudes when you would willingly expel it. For a guest which is unreservedly let in at other seasons and cordially entertained will too frequently break in when you desire to be alone.

The Scriptures are explicit on this subject. It is not merely the committing actual sin that ruins the comfort growing out of prayer; the divine prohibition runs higher. Its interdiction is more intimately interior. It extends to the thoughts and intents of the heart. The door of heaven is shut against prayer under such circumstances. "If I regard iniquity in my heart, the Lord will not hear me." A cherished corruption in the mind is more likely to interpose between

God and the soul because it does not assume the shape and bulk of crime. A practical offense, the effect of sudden temptation, is more likely to be followed by keen repentance, deep self-abasement, and fervent application for pardon; whereas to the close bosom-sin, knowing that no human charge can be brought against it, the soul secretly returns with a fondness facilitated by long indulgence and only whetted by a short separation.

It was, perhaps, this acute experimental feeling which led David to pray to be delivered from "secret sins"; these, he was probably conscious, had led to those "presumptuous sins" which had entangled his soul and embittered his life and whose dominion he so frequently and fervently deprecates. This, it is to be feared, may be the case with some whose language and exterior cause them to be ranked with the religious. These are, at least, the dangers to which they are most exposed. It is, therefore, that our Lord connects, in indissoluble union, watching and prayer.

Perhaps when the conscience is more than usually awakened, you pray with some degree of fervor to be delivered from the guilt and punishment of sin. But if you stop there, your devotion is most imperfect. If you do not also pray to be delivered from its power and dominion over your heart and life, you do not go much farther than the heathens of old. They seem to have had a strong feeling of guilt by their fond desire of expiating it by their sacrifices and lustrations.

But such is the love of present ease and the desire of respite that you think, perhaps, it is better not "to be tormented before the time." How many now in a state of irreversible misery wish they had been tormented sooner that they might not be tormented forever! But with you it is not yet too late. With you the day of grace, which to them is over, is not yet past. Use it, then, without delay, instead of persisting in laying up fresh regrets for eternity.

But too many deceive themselves by imagining that when they have pronounced their prayer, the duty is accomplished with the task; the occult medicine being taken, the charm is to work of itself. They consider it as a duty quite distinct and unconnected with any other. They forget that it is to produce in them a principle which is to mix with all the occurrences of the day. Prayer, though not intended as a talisman, is yet proposed as a remedy. The effect of its operation is to be seen in subduing the passions, assisting to govern the temper, in bridling the tongue, in checking not only calumny but levity, not only impure but vain conversation.

But we have a wonderful talent at deceiving ourselves. We have not a fault for which we do not find an apology. Our ingenuity on this head is inexhaustible. In matters of religion men complain that they are weak, a complaint they are not forward to urge in worldly matters. They lament that their reluctance to pray arises from being unable to do what God, in His Word, expects them to do. But is not this virtual rebellion, only with a smooth face and a soft name? God is too wise not to know exactly what we *can* do and too just to expect from us what we *cannot*.

This pretense of weakness, though it looks like humility, is only a mask for indolence and a screen for selfishness.

We certainly *can* refuse to indulge ourselves in what pleases us when we know it displeases God. We *can* obey His commandments with the aid of the infused strength which He has promised and which we *can* ask. It is not He who is unwilling to give, but we who are averse to pray. The temptations to vice are strengthened by our passions, as our motives to virtue are weakened by them.

Our great spiritual enemy would not be so potent if we ourselves did not put arms into his hands. The world would not be so powerful an enchantress if we did not assist the enchantment by voluntarily yielding to it, by insensibly forsaking Him who is our strength. We make apologies for yielding to both by pleading their power and our own weakness. But the inability to resist is of our own making. Both enemies are indeed powerful, but they are not irresistible. If we assert the contrary, is it not virtually saying, "Greater are they that are against us than He that is for us"?

But we are traitors to our own cause. We are conquered by our own consent. We surrender not so much because the conqueror is powerful as because the conquered is willing.

Without diminishing anything of His grace and glory to whom every good thought we think, every victory over sin we obtain is owing, may it not add to our happiness, even in heaven, to look back on every conquest we here obtained by prayer over our grand spiritual enemy, every triumph over the world, every victory over ourselves? Will not the remembrance of one act of resistance, then, far surpass every gratification now, which the three confederate enemies of our souls may present to us?

It is not merely by our prayers that we must give glory to God. Our divine Master has expressly told us wherein His Father is glorified: It is "when we bring forth much fruit." It is by our works we shall be judged and not by our prayers. And what a final consummation is it that obedience to the will of God, which is our duty here, shall be our nature hereafter! What is now our prayer shall then be our possession. There, the obligation to obey shall become a necessity, and that necessity shall be happiness ineffable.

The various evils here enumerated, with many many others not touched upon, are so many dead weights on the wings of prayer. They cause it to gravitate to earth, obstruct its ascent, and hinder it from piercing to the throne of God.

Chapter VIII

The Lord's Prayer

It is not customary for kings to draw up petitions for their subjects to present to themselves; much less do earthly monarchs consider the act of petitioning worthy of reward, nor do they number the petitions so much among the services done them as among the burdens imposed on them. Whereas it is a singular benefit to our fallen race that the King of kings both dictates our petitions and has promised to recompense us for making them.

In the Lord's Prayer may be found the seminal principle of all the petitions of a Christian, both for spiritual and temporal things; and however in the fullness of his heart he will necessarily depart from his model in his choice of expressions—into whatever laminae he may expand the pure gold of which it is composed—yet he will still find the general principle of his own, more enlarged application to God substantially contained in this brief but finished compendium.

Is it not a striking proof of the divine condescension that, knowing our propensity to err, our blessed Lord should Himself have dictated our petitions, partly perhaps as a corrective of existing superstitions, but certainly to leave behind Him a *regulator* by which all future ages should set their devotions. And we might perhaps establish it as a safe rule for prayer in general that any petition which cannot in some shape be accommodated to the spirit of some part of the Lord's Prayer may not be right to be adopted.

The distinction between the personal nature of Faith, and

the universal character of Charity, as it is exercised in prayer, is specifically exhibited in the two pronouns which stand at the head of the Creed and of the Lord's Prayer. We cannot exercise faith for another and therefore can only say *I* believe. But when we offer up our petitions, we address them to *our* Father, implying that He is the Author, Governor, and Supporter not of ourselves only, but of His whole rational creation. It conveys also a beautiful idea of that boundless charity which links all mankind in one comprehensive brotherhood. The plural *us*, continued through the whole prayer, keeps up the sentiment with which it sets out, tends to exclude selfishness and to excite philanthropy by recommending to God the temporal as well as spiritual wants of the whole family of mankind.

The nomenclature of the Divinity is expressed in Scripture by every term which can convey ideas of grandeur of grace, of power or of affection, of sublimity or tenderness, of majesty or benignity, by every name which can excite terror or trust, which can inspire awe or consolation.

But of all compellations by which the Supreme Being is designated in His holy Word, there is not one so soothing, so attractive, so interesting as that of "Father." It includes the idea of reconciliation, pardon, acceptance, love. It swallows up His grandeur in His beneficence. It involves, also, the inheritance belonging to our filial relation. It fills the mind with every image that is touching, and the heart with every feeling that is affectionate. It inspires fear softened by love and exhibits authority mitigated by tenderness. The most endearing image the psalmist could select from the abundant store-house of his rich conceptions, to convey the kindest sentiment of God's pity toward them that fear Him, was that it resembles the pity of a "father for his *own children.*" In directing us to pray to our Father, our divine Master does not give the command without the example. He everywhere uses the term he recommends: "I thank Thee, O Father, Lord of heaven and earth!" And in the seventeenth chapter of Saint John, he uses this tender name no less than seven times.

"Lord, show us the Father and it sufficeth us," was the ill-understood prayer of the inquiring disciples. To us this petition is granted before it is made. Does He not show Himself to all as a Father, in the wonders of His creation, in the wonders of our being, preservation, and support? Has He not, in a more especial manner revealed Himself to us as a Father in the sublime wonder of His Word, in the unsearchable riches of Christ, and the perpetual gift of the Holy Spirit? Does He not show Himself our Father, if, when we have done evil, He withholds His chastening hand; if, when we have sinned, He still bears with us; if, when we are deaf to His call, He repeats it; if, when we delay, He waits for us; if, when we repent, He pardons us; if, when we return, He receives us; if, when in danger, He preserves us from falling; and if, when we fail, He raises us?

We have a beautiful illustration of the goodness of God as a merciful and tender Father in the deeply affecting parable of the Prodigal Son. Though the undone spendthrift knew that he had no possible claim on the goodness he had so notoriously offended, yet he felt that the endearing name of Father had an eloquence that might plead for forgiveness of his offense, though, he feared, not for restoration to affection and favor. But while he only meekly aspired to a place among the servants, while he only humbly pleaded for a little of their redundant bread, he was received as a pardoned, reconciled, beloved child.

Our Lord's introduction, "Pray ye therefore after this *manner*," neither forbids digression nor amplification. The recollection that his dwelling place is in heaven is calculated to remind us of the immeasurable distance between the petitioner and his God, and to encourage us to communicate with the Father of Spirits, with Him who is "glorious in holiness, fearful in praises, doing wonders." And which of His wonders is more astonishing than this inconceivably marvelous condescension?

Christianity, we must repeat, is a practical religion, and in order to use aright the prayer our Lord has given us, we must model our life by it as well as our petitions.

If we pray that the name of God may be hallowed, yet neglect to hallow it ourselves, by family as well as personal devotion and a conscientious attendance on all the ordinances of public worship, we defeat the end of our praying by falling short of its obligation.

The discrepancies between our prayers and our practice do not end here. How frequently are we solemnly imploring of God that "his kingdom may come," while we are doing nothing to promote His kingdom of grace here and consequently His kingdom of glory hereafter.

If we pray that God would "give His Son the heathen for His inheritance" and yet make it a matter of indifference, whether a vast proportion of the globe should live heathens or die Christians; if we pray that "the knowledge of the Lord may cover the earth, as the waters cover the sea" yet act as if we were indifferent whether Christianity ended as well as began at home; if we pray that "the sound may go out into all lands, and their words unto the ends of the world" and yet are satisfied to keep the sound within our own island— is not this a prayer which goeth out of feigned lips? When we pray that "his will may be done," we know that His will is that "all should be saved, that no one should perish." When, therefore, we assist in sending the Gospel to the dark and distant corners of the earth, then, and not till then, may we consistently desire of God in our prayers that "his saving health may be known to all nations."

In praying, therefore, that "his kingdom may come," do we not pray that all false religions, all idolatrous worship may be universally abolished and the kingdom of Messiah be established throughout the world?

If praying for our "daily bread" is a petition expressing our dependence, it is also a petition of temperance. It teaches us to subordinate our desires after worldly things and to ask for them in great moderation. It is worth observing that requests for temporal blessings and spiritual mercies are so interwoven in this perfect form that in repeating it, we cannot pray for our "daily bread" without imploring "forgiveness of our trespasses."

"Deliverance from evil" is a petition of indefinite extent and is closely connected with that which precedes it. God cannot "lead us into temptation," but His Providence may lead us into situations which, acting on the corruption of our hearts, may eventually produce the evil we deprecate.

When we pray, therefore, not to be "led into temptation," we are asking of God to cure those sinful propensities which are likely to expose us to it and to preserve us from those circumstances which, by subjecting us to difficulty and danger, may terminate in sin.

Temptation, in the language of Scripture, frequently implies probation, a trial sent in order to lay open our real character. Thus God, in tempting Abraham, gave occasion to that illustrious exemplification of faith and obedience in this devoted Patriarch. God is also said to try Hezekiah. This trial led him into the vain display of magnificence and wealth before the foreign ambassadors. The Searcher of hearts already knew this infirmity, yet it is said by the sacred historians that "God left him to try him, that He might know all that was in his heart." Doubtless the public exposure of his pride was calculated to lead Hezekiah to subsequent repentance and humility; for, in spite of this error he was eminently conspicuous among the awfully few pious kings of Judah.

There is in the Lord's Prayer a concatenation of the several clauses, what in human composition the critics call concealed method. The petitions rise out of each other. Every part also is, as it were, fenced round the whole meeting in a circle, for the desire that God's name may be hallowed, His will be done, and His kingdom come, with which the prayer opens, is referred to and confirmed by the ascription at the close. If the kingdom, the power, and the glory are His, then His ability to do and to give is declared to be infinite.

Chapter IX

The Lord's Prayer Continued—"Thy Will Be Done"

The Holy Scriptures frequently comprise the essence of the Christian temper in some short aphorism, apostrophe, or definition. The essential spirit of the Christian life may be said to be included in this one brief petition of the Lord's Prayer: "Thy will be done."

There is a haughty spirit which, though it will not complain, does not care to submit. It arrogates to itself the dignity of enduring, without any claim to the meekness of yielding. Its silence is stubbornness. Its fortitude is pride. Its calmness is apathy without and discontent within. In such characters it is not so much the will of God which is the role of conduct as the scorn of pusillanimity. Not seldom, indeed, the mind puts in a claim for a merit to which the nerves could make out a better title. Yet the suffering which arises from acute feeling is so far from deducting from the virtue of resignation that, when it does not impede the sacrifice, it enhances the value. True resignation is the hardest lesson in the whole school of Christ. It is the oftenest taught and the latest learnt. It is not a task which, when once got over in some particular instance, leaves us master of the subject. The necessity of following up the lesson we have begun presents itself almost every day in some new shape, occurs under some fresh modification. The submission of yesterday does not exonerate us from the resignation of today. The principle, indeed, once thoroughly wrought into the soul, gradually reconciles us to the frequent demand for its exercise and renders every successive call more easy.

We read dissertations on this subject, not only with the most entire concurrence of the judgment, but with the most apparent conviction of the mind. We write essays upon it in the hour of peace and composure, and fancy that what we have discussed with so much ease and self-complacence, in favor of which we offer so many arguments to convince and so many motives to persuade, cannot be very difficult to practise. But to convince the understanding and to correct the will is a very different undertaking, and not less difficult when it comes to our own case than it was in the case of those for whom we have been so coolly and dogmatically prescribing. It is not till we practically find how slowly our own arguments produce any effect on ourselves that we cease to marvel at their inefficacy on others. The sick physician tastes with disgust the bitterness of the draught, to the swallowing of which he wondered the patient had felt so much repugnance. And the reader is sometimes convinced by the arguments which fail of their effect on the writer when he is called not to discuss but to act, not to reason but to suffer. The theory is so just and the duty so obvious that even bad men assent to it; the exercise so trying that the best men find it more easy to commend the rule than to adopt it. But he who has once gotten engraved, not in his memory, but in his heart, this divine precept, "Thy will be done," has made a proficiency which will render all subsequent instruction comparatively easy.

Though sacrifices and oblations were offered to God under the law by His own express appointment, yet He peremptorily rejected them by His prophets when presented as substitute instead of signs. Will he, under a more perfect dispensation, accept any observances which are meant to supersede internal dedication, any offerings unaccompanied by complete desire of acquiescence in His will? "My son, give me thine *heart*" is His brief but imperative command. But before we can be brought to comply with the spirit of this requisition, God must enlighten our understanding, that our devotion may be rational; He must rectify our will, that it may be voluntary; He must purify our heart, that it may be spiritual.

Submission is a duty of such high and holy import that it can only be learnt of the Great Teacher. If it could have been acquired by mere moral institution, the wise sayings of the ancient philosophers would have taught it. But their most elevated standard was low. Their strongest motives were the brevity of life, the instability of fortune, the dignity of suffering virtue, things within their narrow sphere of judging; things true, indeed, as far as they go, but a substratum by no means equal to the superstructure to be built on it. It wanted depth and strength and solidity for the purposes of support. It wanted the only true basis, the assurance that God orders all things according to the purposes of His will for our final good. It wanted that only sure ground of faith by which the genuine Christian cheerfully submits in entire dependence on the promises of the Gospel.

Nor let us fancy that we are to be languid and inactive recipients of the divine dispensations. Our own souls must be enlarged, our own views must be ennobled, our own spirit must be dilated. An inoperative acquiescence is not all that is required of us. And if we must not slacken our zeal in doing good, so we must not be remiss in opposing evil on the flimsy ground that God has permitted evil to infest the world. If it be His will to permit sin, it is an opposition to His will when we do not labor to counteract it. This surrender, therefore, of our will to that of God takes in a large sweep of actual duties, as well as the whole compass of passive obedience. It involves doing as well as suffering, activity as well as acquiescence, zeal as well as forbearance. Yet the concise petition daily slips off the tongue without our reflecting on the weight of the obligation we are imposing on ourselves. We do not consider the extent and consequences of the prayer we are offering, the sacrifices, the trials, the privations it may involve, and the large indefinite obedience to all the known and unknown purposes of Infinite Wisdom to which we are pledging ourselves.

There is no case in which we more shelter ourselves in generalities. Verbal sacrifices cost little, cost nothing. The familiar habit of repeating the petition almost tempts us to fancy that the duty is as easy as the request is short. We are ready to think that a prayer rounded off in four monosyllables can scarcely involve duties co-extensive with our whole course of being; that in uttering them we renounce all right in ourselves; that we acknowledge the universal indefeasible title of *the blessed and only Potentate;* that we make over to Him the right to do in us and with us and by us whatever He sees good for ourselves, whatever will promote His glory, though by means sometimes as incomprehensible to our understanding, as unacceptable to our will, because we neither know the motive nor perceive the end. These simple words, "Thy will be done," express an act of faith the most sublime, an act of allegiance the most unqualified; and while they make a declaration of entire submission to a sovereign the most absolute, they are at the same time a recognition of love to a Father the most beneficent.

We must remember that in offering this prayer, we may, by our own request, be offering to resign what we most dread to lose, to give up what is dear to us as our own soul. We may be calling on our heavenly Father to withhold what we are most anxiously laboring to attain and to withdraw what we are most sedulously endeavoring to keep. We are solemnly renouncing our property in ourselves; we are distinctly making ourselves over again to Him whose we already are. We specifically entreat Him to do with us what He pleases, to mold us to a conformity to His image, without which we shall never be resigned to His will; in short, to dispose of us as His infinite wisdom sees best, however contrary to the scheme which our blindness has laid down as the path to unquestionable happiness.

To render this trying petition easy to us is one great reason why God, by such a variety of providences, afflicts and brings us low. He knows that we want incentives to humility even more than incitements to virtuous actions.

He shows us in many ways that self-sufficiency and happiness are incompatible, that pride and peace are irreconcilable, that following our own way and doing our own will, which we conceive to be the very essence of felicity, are in direct opposition to it.

Under the pressure of any affliction, "Thy will be done," as it is the patient Christian's unceasing prayer, so it is the ground of his unvarying practice. In this brief petition he finds his whole duty comprised and expressed. It is the unprompted request of his lips; it is the motto inscribed on his heart; it is the principle which regulates his life; it is the voice which says to the stormy passion, "Peace! be still!" Let others expostulate, he submits. Nay, even submission does not adequately express his feelings. We frequently submit not so much from duty as from necessity. We submit because we cannot help ourselves. Resignation sometimes may be mere acquiescence in the sovereignty, rather than conviction of the wisdom and goodness of God, while the patient Christian not only yields to the dispensation, but adores the dispenser. He not only submits to the blow, but vindicates the hand which inflicts it: "The Lord is righteous in all His ways." He refers to the chastisement as a proof of the affection of the chastiser: "I know that in very faithfulness Thou hast caused me to be afflicted." He recurs to the thoughtlessness of his former prosperity: "Before I was afflicted I went astray." And he alludes to the trial less as a punishment than a paternal correction. If he prays for a removal of the present suffering, he prays also that it may not be removed from him till it has been sanctified to him. He will not even part from the trial till he has laid hold on the benefit.

"Christianity," says Bishop Horsley, "involves many paradoxes, but no contradictions." To be able to say with entire surrender of the heart, "Thy will be done," is the true liberty of the children of God, that liberty with which Christ has made us free. It is a liberty, not which delivers us from restraint, but which, freeing us from our subjection to the senses, makes us find no pleasure but in order, no safety but in the obedience of an intelligent being to his rightful

Lord. In delivering us from the heavy bondage of sin, it transfers us to the "easy yoke of Christ," from the galling slavery of the world to the "light burden of Him who overcame it."

This liberty, in giving a true direction to the affections, gives them amplitude as well as elevation. The more unconstrained the will becomes, the more it fixes on one object; once fixed on the highest, it does not use its liberty for versatility, but for consistency; not for change, but fidelity; not for wavering, but adherence.

It is, therefore, no less our interest than our duty to keep the mind in an habitual posture of submission. "Adam," says Dr. Hammond, "after his expulsion, was a greater slave in the wilderness than he had been in the enclosure." If the barbarian ambassador came expressly to the Romans to negotiate from his country for permission to be their servants, declaring that a voluntary submission even to a foreign power was preferable to a wild and disorderly freedom, well may the Christian triumph in the peace and security to be attained by a complete subjugation to Him who is emphatically called *the God of order.*

A vital faith manifests itself in vital acts. "Thy will be done," is eminently a practical petition. The first indication of the jailer's change of heart was a practical indication. He did not ask, "Are there few that be saved?" but, "What shall I do to be saved?" The first symptom Saint Paul gave of his conversion was a practical symptom: "Lord, what wilt Thou have me to do?" He entered on his new course with a total renunciation of his own will. It seemed to this great apostle to be the turning point between infidelity and piety, whether he should follow his own will or the will of God. He did not amuse his curiosity with speculative questions. His own immediate and grand concern engrossed his whole soul. Nor was his question a mere hasty effusion, an interrogative springing out of that mixed feeling of awe and wonder which accompanied his first overwhelming convictions. It became the abiding principle which governed his future life, which made him in labors more abundant. Every successive act of duty, every future sacrifice of ease sprung from it, was influenced by it. His own will, his ardent, impetuous, fiery will, was not merely subdued; it was extinguished. His powerful mind indeed lost none of its energy, but his proud heart relinquished all its independence.

We allow and adopt the term *devotion* as an indispensable part of religion, because it is supposed to be limited to the act; but *devotedness*, from which it is derived, does not meet with such ready acceptation, because this is a habit, and a habit involves more than an act; it pledges us to consistency; it implies fixedness of character, a general confirmed state of mind, a giving up what we are and have and do to God. Devotedness does not consist in the length of our prayers, nor in the number of our good works, for, though these are the surest evidences of piety, they are not its essence. Devotedness consists in doing and suffering, bearing and forbearing in the way which God prescribes. The most inconsiderable duty performed with alacrity, if it opposes our own inclination, the most ordinary trial, met with a right spirit is more acceptable to Him than a greater effort of our own devising. We do not commend a servant for his activity, if ever so fervently exercised, in doing whatever gratifies his own fancy. We do not consider his performance as obedience, unless his activity has been exercised in doing what we required of him. Now, how can we insist on his doing what contradicts his own humor, while we allow ourselves to feel repugnance in serving our heavenly Master, when His commands do not exactly fall in with our own inclination?

Nothing short, then, of this sincere devotedness to God can enable us to maintain an equality of mind under unequal circumstances. We murmur that we have not the things we ask amiss, not knowing that they are withheld by the same mercy by which the things that are good for us are granted. Things good in themselves may not be good for us. A resigned spirit is the proper disposition to prepare us for receiving mercies or for having them denied. Resignation of soul, like the allegiance of a good subject, is always in readiness, though not always in action; whereas an impatient mind is a spirit of disaffection, always prepared to revolt when the will of the sovereign is in opposition to that of the subject. This seditious principle is the infallible characteristic of an unrenewed mind.

We must also give God leave not only to take His own way, but His own time. The appointment of seasons, as well as of events, is his. "He waits to be gracious." If He delays, it is because we are not yet brought to that state which fits us for the grant of our request. It is not He who must be brought about, but we ourselves. Or perhaps He refuses the thing we ask in order to give us a better. We implore success in an undertaking, instead of which, He gives us content under the disappointment. We ask for the removal of pain; He gives us patience under it. We desire deliverance from our enemies; He sees that we have not yet turned their enmity to our improvement, and He will bring us to a better temper by further exercise. We desire Him to avert some impending trial; instead of averting it, He takes away its bitterness. He mitigates what we believed would be intolerable by giving us a right temper under it. How, then, can we say He has failed of His promise if He gives something more truly valuable than we had requested at His hands?

A sincere love of God will make us thankful when our prayers are granted and patient and cheerful when they are denied. Every fresh disappointment will teach us to distrust ourselves and confide in God. Experience will instruct us that there may be a better way of hearing our requests than that of granting them. Happy for us that He to whom they are addressed knows what is best and acts upon that knowledge.

Chapter X

A Slight Scheme of Prayer Proposed for Young Persons on the Model of the Lord's Prayer

Will the pious mother pardon the liberty here taken of suggesting the few following hints? Those who are aware of the inestimable value of prayer themselves will naturally be anxious not only that this duty should be earnestly inculcated on their children, but that they should be taught it in the best manner. And *such* parents need little persuasion or counsel on the subject. Yet children of decent and orderly (I will not say of strictly religious) families are often so superficially instructed in this important business that when they are asked what prayers they use, it is not unusual for them to answer, "The Lord's Prayer and the *Creed*." And even some who are better taught are not always made to understand with sufficient clearness the specific distinction between the two, that the one is the confession of their *faith* and the other the model for their *supplications.* By this confused and indistinct beginning, they set out with a perplexity in their ideas which is not always completely disentangled in more advanced life.

An intelligent mother will seize the first occasion which the child's opening understanding shall allow for making a little course of lectures on the Lord's Prayer, taking every division or short sentence separately, for each furnishes valuable materials for a distinct lecture. Children should be led gradually through every part of this divine composition. They should be taught to break it into regular divisions into which, indeed, it so naturally resolves itself. They should be made to comprehend, one by one, each of its short but weighty sentences, to amplify and spread them out for the purpose of better understanding them, not in their most extensive and critical sense, but in their most simple and obvious meanings. For in these condensed and substantial expressions, as we have before observed, every word is an ingot and will bear beating out, so that the teacher's difficulty will not so much be what she shall say as what she shall suppress, so abundant is the expository matter which this succinct pattern suggests.

When children have acquired a pretty good conception of the meaning of each division, they should then be made to observe the connection, relation, and dependence of the several parts of this Prayer, one upon another, for there is great method and connection in it. A judicious interpreter will observe how logically and consequently one clause grows out of another, though she will use neither the word logically nor consequence; for all explanations should be made in the most plain and familiar terms, it being words and not things which commonly perplex children, if, as it sometimes happens, the teacher, though not wanting sense, wants perspicuity and simplicity.

Young persons, from being completely instructed in this short composition (which, as it is to be their guide and model through life, too much pains cannot be bestowed on it), will have a clearer conception not only of its individual contents, but of prayer in general, than many ever attain, though their memory has been, perhaps, loaded with long and unexplained forms which they have been accustomed to swallow in the lump without scrutiny and without discrimination.

I would have it understood that by these little comments I do not mean that children should be put to learn dry and, to them, unintelligible expositions, but that the exposition is to be colloquial. And here I must remark in general that the teacher is sometimes unreasonably apt to relieve herself at the child's expense by loading the *memory* of a little creature on occasions in which far other faculties should be put in exercise. Children themselves should be made to furnish a good part of this extemporaneous commentary by their answers, in which answers they will be much assisted by the judgment the teacher uses in her manner of questioning. And the youthful understanding, when its powers are properly set at work, will soon strengthen by exercise so as to furnish reasonable, if not very correct, answers.

Written forms of prayer are not only useful and proper, but indispensably necessary to begin with. But I will hazard the remark that if children are thrown *exclusively* on the best forms, if they are made to commit them to memory like a copy of verses and to repeat them in a dry, customary way, they will produce little effect on their minds. They will not understand what they repeat if we do not early open to them the important *scheme* of prayer. Without such an elementary introduction to this duty, they will afterward be either ignorant or enthusiastic in both. We should give them *knowledge* before we can expect them to make much progress in *piety,* and as a due preparative to it; Christian instruction in this resembling the sun, who, in the course of his communication, gives light before he gives heat. And to labor to excite a spirit of devotion without first infusing that knowledge out of which it is to grow is practically reviving the [once traditional] maxim that ignorance is the mother of Devotion, and virtually adopting the [ecclesiastical] rule of praying in an unknown tongue.

Children, let me again observe, will not attend to their prayers if they do not understand them, and they will not understand them if they are not taught to analyze, to dissect them, to know their component parts, and to methodize them.

It is not enough to teach them to consider prayer under the general idea that it is an application to God for what they want and an acknowledgment to Him for what they have. This, though true in the gross, is not sufficiently precise and correct. They should learn to define and to arrange all the different parts of prayer. And as a preparative to prayer itself, they should be impressed with as clear an idea as their capacity and the nature of the subject will admit, of Him with whom they have to do. His omnipresence is perhaps of all His attributes that of which we may make the first practical use. Every head of prayer is founded on some great Scriptural truths, which truths the little analysis here suggested will maternally assist to fix in their minds.

On the knowledge that "God is," that He is an infinitely holy Being, and that "He is the rewarder of all them that diligently seek Him," will be grounded the first part of prayer, which is *adoration.* The creature devoting itself to the Creator, or *self-dedication* next presents itself. And if they are first taught that important truth, that as needy creatures they want help, which may be done by some easy analogy, they will easily be led to understand how naturally *petition* forms a most considerable branch of prayer; and divine grace being among the things for which they are to petition, this naturally suggests to the mind the doctrine of the influences of the Holy Spirit. And when to this is added the conviction which will be readily worked into an ingenuous mind that as offending creatures they want pardon, the necessity of *confession* will easily be made intelligible to them. But they should be brought to understand that it must not be such a general and vague confession as awakens no sense of personal humiliation, as excites no recollection of their own more peculiar and individual faults. But it must be a confession founded on self-knowledge, which is itself to arise out of the practice of self-examination. On the gladness of heart natural to youth, it will be less difficult to impress the delightful duty of *thanksgiving,* which forms so considerable a branch of prayer. In this they should be habituated to recapitulate not only their general, but to enumerate their peculiar, daily, and incidental mercies in the same specific manner as they should have been taught to detail their individual and personal *wants* in the petitionary, and their *faults* in the confessional part. The same warmth of feeling which will more readily dispose them to express their gratitude to God in thanksgiving will also lead them more gladly to express their love to their parents and friends by adopting another indispensable and, to an affectionate heart, pleasing part of prayer, which is *intercession*. It will be needful to inform them that the omission of this important clause in the *Lord's Prayer* arises from the divine Intercessor not having then assumed His mediatorial office.

When they have been made, by a plain and perspicuous mode of instruction, fully to understand the different nature of all these, and when they clearly comprehend that *adoration, self-dedication, confession, petition, thanksgiving,* and *intercession* are distinct heads which must not be involved in each other, you may exemplify the rules by pointing out to them these successive branches in any well-written form. It is hardly needful to remind the teacher that our truly Scriptural Liturgy invariably furnishes the example of presenting *every* request in the name of the great Mediator. For there is no access to the Throne of Grace but by *that new and living way.* In the Liturgy too they will meet with the best exemplifications of prayers, exhibiting separate specimens of each of the distinct heads we have been suggesting.

But in order that the minds of young persons may without labor or difficulty be gradually brought into such a state of preparation as to be benefited by such a little course of lectures as we have recommended, they should, from the time when they were first able to read, have been employing themselves, at their leisure hours, in laying in a store of provision for their present demands. And here the memory may be employed to good purpose; for being the first faculty which is ripened and which is indeed perfected when the others are only beginning to unfold themselves, this is an intimation of Providence that it should be the first seized on for the best uses. It should therefore be devoted to lay in a stock of the more easy and devotional parts of Scripture, especially the Psalms.* Children whose minds have been early well furnished from these will be competent at nine or ten years old to produce from them, and to select with no contemptible judgment, suitable examples of all the parts of prayer, and will be able to extract and appropriate texts under each respective head so as to exhibit, without help, complete specimens of every part of prayer. By confining them entirely to the sense and nearly to the words of Scripture, they will be preserved from enthusiasm, from irregularity and conceit. By being obliged continually to apply for themselves, they will get a habit in all their difficulties, of "searching the Scriptures," which may be hereafter useful to them on other and more trying occasions. But I would at first *confine* them to the Bible, for were they allowed with equal freedom to ransack other books with a view to get helps to embellish their little compositions, or rather compilations, they might be tempted to pass off for their own what they pick up from others, which might tend at once make them both vain and deceitful. This is a temptation to which they are too much laid open when they find themselves extravagantly commended for any pilfered passage with which they decorate their little themes and letters. But in the present instance there is no danger of any similar deception, for there is such a sacred signature stamped on every Scripture phrase that the owner's name can never be defaced or torn off from the goods either by fraud or violence.

It would be well, if in those Psalms which children were first directed to get by heart an eye were had to this their future application, and that they were employed, but without any intimation of your subsequent design, in learning such as may be best turned to this account. In the

---

*This will be so far from spoiling the cheerfulness or impeding the pleasures of childhood that the Author knows a lady who, when a little girl, before she was seven years old, had learnt the whole Psalter through a second time, and that without any diminution of uncommon gaiety of spirits or any interference with the elegant acquirements suited to her station.

hundred and thirty-ninth Psalm, the first great truth to be imprinted on the young heart, the divine omnipresence, as was before observed, is unfolded with such a mixture of majestic grandeur and such an interesting variety of intimate and local circumstances as is likely to seize on the quick and lively feeling of youth. The awful idea that that Being whom they are taught to reverence is not only *in general* "acquainted with all their ways," but that He is "about their path, and about their bed," bestows such a sense of real and present existence on Him, of whom they are apt to conceive as having His distant habitation only in heaven, as will greatly help to realize the sense of His actual presence.

The hundred and third Psalm will open to the mind rich and abundant sources of expression for gratitude and thanksgiving, and it includes the acknowledgment of spiritual as well as temporal favors. It illustrates the compassionate mercies of God by familiar tenderness and exquisite endearment, as are calculated to strike upon every chord of filial fondness in the heart of an affectionate child. The fifty-first supplies an infinite variety of matter in whatever relates to confession of sin or to supplication for the aide of the Spirit. The twenty-third abounds with captivating expressions of the protecting goodness and tender love of their heavenly Father, conveyed by pastoral imagery of uncommon beauty and sweetness. In short, the greater part of these charming compositions overflows with materials for every head of prayer.

Children who, while they were engaged in learning these Scriptures, were not aware that there was any specific object in view or any farther end to be answered by it will afterward feel an unexpected pleasure arising from the application of their petty labors, when they are called to draw out from their little treasury of knowledge the stores they have been insensibly collecting, and will be pleased to find that, without any fresh application to study, they are now obliged to exercise a higher faculty than memory; they have lying ready in their minds the materials with which they are at length called upon to work. Their judgment must be set about selecting one or two or more texts which shall contain the substance of every specific head of prayer before noticed; and it will be a farther exercise to their understandings to concatenate the detached parts into one regular whole, occasionally varying the arrangement as they like; that is, changing the order, sometimes beginning with invocation, sometimes with confession, sometimes dwelling longer on one part, sometimes on another. As the hardships of a religious Sunday are often so pathetically pleaded as making one of the heavy burdens of religion, and as the friends of religion are so often called upon to mitigate its intolerable rigors by recommending pleasant employment, might not such an exercise as has been here suggested assist, by varying its occupations, to lighten its load!

The habits of the pupils being thus early formed, their memory, attention, and intellect being bent in a rigid direction, and the exercise invariably maintained, may we not reasonably hope that their *affections* also, through divine grace, may become interested in the work, till they will be enabled "to pray with the spirit, and with the understanding also"? They will now be qualified to use a well-composed form with seriousness and advantage, for they will now use it not mechanically, but rationally. That which before appeared to them a mere mass of good words will now appear a significant composition, exhibiting variety, regularity, and beauty; and while they will have the further advantage of being enabled, by their improved judgment, to distinguish and select for their own purpose such prayers as are more judicious and more scriptural, it will also habituate them to look for plan and design and lucid order in other works.

Chapter XI

Of Perseverance in Prayer and Praise

A deep sense of his corruptions will powerfully draw the real penitent to a humble avowal of sin; but it is to be feared that there are some, who, because they cannot charge themselves with flagrant offenses, do not consider a contrite confession of the sins of the heart and of the daily life an indispensable part of their devotions. But God will charge many with sin who neglect to charge themselves. Did they attend to the remonstrances of a conscience not laid asleep by neglect or quieted by palliatives, they would find that, were the daily *omissions* alone, whether in prayer or conduct, of even their best days registered and presented to them, they would form no inconsiderable catalog for repentance.

There are too many who do not consider that all sins are equally a breach of the divine law. Without pretending to bring all sins, small and great, to one common level, we should remember that *all* sin is an offense against a gracious Father.

In that profoundly self-abasing prayer of David, after the commission of the two black offenses which disgraced his otherwise exemplary life, though he deeply felt his barbarous treatment of his brave general, in first dishonoring his wife, and then exposing him to meet inevitable death in the forefront of the hottest battle—yet in praying to be delivered from this "blood-guiltiness," he bequeathed an important lesson to posterity when in his lowly prostration at the throne of God, his first cry was, "Against *Thee, Thee* only, have I sinned, and done this evil in *Thy* sight," plainly declaring that all sin is, in the first instance, a sin against God.

While the most worldly are ready enough to exclaim against notorious sins or against any sins carried to the greatest excess, to smaller offenses they contrive to be tolerably reconciled. They think the commission of these not inconsistent with the profitable use of prayer in their formal way of using this customary exercise.

They are also sufficiently lenient to certain degrees of great sins, and various are the modifications and distinctions in their logic, and not overcorrect the gradations in their moral scale of degrees. They do not consider that it is the extirpation and not merely the reduction of any sin which is to procure them that peace and comfort for which they sometimes pray and which they wonder they do not receive as an answer to their prayers.

They forget that the evil of sin is not to be measured by its magnitude only, but by the spirit of disobedience which it indicates toward a generous Father, a Father whose commands are all founded in mercy and love, and who considers every voluntary fault as no light offense when committed against supreme power exercised with perfect tenderness.

But it is their reluctance to part with the remaining degrees, their wish to retain these modified sins; it is their favorite reserves, to which they still cling, that prevent that peace which is promised to the victory, I had almost said to the omnipotence, of prayer.

For it is not so much the nicely measured quantity as to the nature of sin which constitutes its malignity and instructs the benefit of prayer. The inferior degree which is cherished, will, without earnest supplication to God, be ready to become the excess which is deprecated, whenever the appropriate temptation shall present itself. For however our compassionate Father may pardon the unpremeditated fault, yet how can we expect Him to forgive any degree of sin that is allowed, that is even in a certain measure, intended to be committed? Diminution, however, is a favorable step, if, by perseverance in prayer, it lead gradually to extirpation. And this naturally leads to the important subject of perseverance in prayer.

Prayer is an act which seems to be so prepared in the frame of our nature; to be so congenial to our dependent condition; so suited to our exigencies; so adapted to every man's known wants and to his possibilities of wants unknown; so full of relief to the soul and of peace to the mind and of gladness to the heart; so productive of confidence in God; and so reciprocally preceding from that confidence, that we should think, if we did not know the contrary, that it is a duty which scarcely required to be enjoined; that he who had once found out his necessities, and that there was no other redress for them, would spontaneously have recourse, as a delight, to what he had neglected as a command; that he who had once tasted the bounties of God, would think it a hardship not to be allowed to thank Him for them; that the invitation to pray to his Benefactor was an additional proof of divine goodness; that to be allowed to praise Him for the mercies, was itself a mercy.

The apostle's precept "Pray always" (pray evermore, pray without ceasing, men ought always to pray) will not be criticized as a pleonasm if we call to remembrance that there is no state of mind, no condition of life in which prayer is not a necessity as well as an obligation. In danger, fear impels to it; in trouble, we have no other resource; in sickness, we have no other refuge; in dejection, no other hope in death, no other comfort.

Saint Paul frequently shows the word *prayer* to be a term of great latitude, involving the whole compass of our intercourse with God. He represents it to include our adoration of His perfections; our acknowledgment of the wisdom of His dispensations; our obligation for His benefits, providential and spiritual; the avowal of our entire dependence on Him; our absolute subjection to Him; the declaration of our faith in Him; the expression of our devotedness to Him; the confession of our own unworthiness, infirmities, and sins; the petition for the supply of our wants, and for the pardon of our offenses; for succor in our distress; for a blessing on our undertakings; for the direction of our conduct, and the success of our affairs.

If any should be disposed to think this general view too comprehensive, let him point out which of these particulars prayer does not embrace, which of these clauses a rational, a sentient, an enlightened, a dependent being can omit in his scheme of devotion.

But as the multifarious concerns of human life will necessarily occasion a suspension of the exercise, the apostle, ever attentive to the principle of the act and to the circumstances of the actor, reduces all these qualities to their essence when he resolves them into *the spirit* of supplication.

To pray incessantly, therefore, appears to be, in his view of the subject, to keep the mind in an habitual disposition and propensity to devotion. For there is a sense in which we may be said to *do* that which we are *willing* to do, though there are intervals of the thought as well as intermissions of the act, "as a traveler," says Dr. Barrow, "may be said to be still on his journey, though he stops to take needful rest, and to transact necessary business." If he pause, he does not turn out of the way; his pursuit is not diverted, though occasionally interrupted.

Constantly maintaining the disposition, then, and never neglecting the actual duty, never slighting the occasion which presents itself, nor violating the habit of stated devotion, may we presume, be called "to pray without ceasing." The expression "watching unto prayer" implies this vigilance in finding and this zeal in laying hold on these occasions.

The success of prayer, though promised to all who offer it in perfect sincerity, is not so frequently promised to the cry of distress, to the impulse of fear, or the emergency of the moment, as to humble continuance in devotion. It is to patient waiting, to assiduous solicitation, to unwearied importunity that God has declared that He will lend His ear, that He will give the communication of His Spirit, that He will grant the return of our requests. Nothing but this holy perseverance can keep up in our minds a humble sense of our dependence. It is not by a mere casual petition, however passionate, but by habitual application that devout affections are excited and maintained, that our converse with heaven is carried on. It is by no other means that we can be assured, with Saint Paul, that "we are risen with Christ," but this obvious one, that we thus seek the things which are above; that the heart is renovated; that the mind is lifted above this low scene of things; that the spirit breathes in a purer atmosphere; that the whole man is enlightened and strengthened and purified; and that the most frequently, so the more nearly, he approaches to the throne of God. He will find also that prayer not only expresses but elicits the divine grace.

Yet do we not allow every idle plea, every frivolous pretense to divert us from our better resolves? Business brings in its grave apology; pleasure its bewitching excuse. But if we would examine our hearts truly and report them faithfully, we should find the fact to be that disinclination to this employment, oftener than our engagement in any other, keeps us from this sacred intercourse with our Maker.

Under circumstances of distress, indeed, prayer is adopted with comparatively little reluctance. The mind which knows not where to fly flies to God. In agony, nature is no atheist. The soul is drawn to God by a sort of natural impulse, not always, perhaps, by an emotion of piety, but from a feeling conviction that every other refuge is a "refuge of lies." Oh! Thou afflicted, tossed with tempests and not comforted, happy if thou art either drawn or driven, with holy David, to say to thy God, "Thou art a place to hide me in."

But if it is easy for the sorrowing heart to give up a world, by whom itself seems to be given up, there are other demands for prayer equally imperative. There are circumstances more dangerous, yet less suspected of danger, in which, though the call is louder, it is less heard, because the voice of conscience is drowned by the clamors of the world. Prosperous fortunes, unbroken health, flattering friends, buoyant spirits, a springtide of success—these are the occasions when the very abundance of God's mercies is apt to fill the heart till it hardens it. Loaded with riches, crowned with dignities, successful in enterprise, beset with snares in the shape of honors, with perils under the mask of pleasure—then it is, that to the already saturated heart "tomorrow shall be as this day, and more abundant," is more in unison than "what shall I render to the Lord?"

Prayer draws all the Christian graces into its focus. It draws Charity, followed by her lovely train, her forbearance with faults, her forgiveness of injuries, her pity for errors, her compassion for want. It draws Repentance, with her holy sorrows, her pious resolution, her self-distrust. It attracts Faith, with her elevated eye; Hope, with her grasped anchor; Beneficence with her open hand; Zeal, looking far and wide to serve; Humility, with introverted eye, looking at home. Prayer, by quickening these graces in the heart, warms them into life, fits them for service, and dismisses each to its appropriate practice. Prayer is mental virtue; virtue is spiritual action. The mold into which genuine prayer casts the soul is not effaced by the suspension of the act, but retains some touches of the impression till the act is repeated.

When we consider how profusely God bestows and how little He requires; that while He confers like Deity, He desires only such poor returns as can be made by indigent, mendicant mortality; that He requires no costly oblation, nothing that will impoverish but, on the contrary, will inconceivably enrich the giver—when we consider this, we are ready to wonder that He will accept so poor a thing as impotent gratitude for immeasurable bounty. When we reflect that our very desire to pray and to praise Him is His gift; that His grace must purify the offering before He condescends to receive it, must confer on it that spirit which renders it acceptable; that He only expects we should consecrate to Him what we have received from Him; that we should only confess; that of all we enjoy, nothing is our due—we may well blush at our insensibility.

We think, perhaps, that had He commanded us "to do

some great thing," to raise some monument of splendor, some memorial of notoriety and ostentation, something that would perpetuate our own name with His goodness, we should gladly have done it. How much more when He only requires

"Our thanks how due!"

when He only asks the homage of the heart, the expression of our dependence, the recognition of His right!

But he to whom the duty of prayer is unknown and by whom the privilege of prayer is unfelt, or he by whom it is neglected, or he who uses it for form and not from feeling, may probably say, "Will this work, wearisome even if necessary, never know an end? Will there be no period when God will dispense with its regular exercise? Will there never be such an attainment of the end proposed, as that we may be allowed to discontinue the means?"

To these interrogatories there is but one answer, an answer which shall be also made by an appeal to the enquirer himself.

If there is any day in which we are quite certain that we shall meet with no trial from Providence, no temptation from the world, any day in which we shall be sure to have no wrong tempers excited in ourselves, no call to bear with those of others, no misfortune to encounter, and no need of divine assistance to endure it, on that morning we may safely omit prayer.

If there is any evening in which we have received no protection from God and experienced no mercy at His hands, if we have not lost a single opportunity of doing or receiving good, if we are quite certain that we have not once spoken unadvisedly with our lips, nor entertained one vain or idle thought in our heart, on that night we may safely omit to praise God and to confess our own sinfulness; on that night we may safely omit humiliation and thanksgiving. To repeat the converse would be superfluous.

When we can conscientiously say that religion has given a tone to our conduct, a law to our actions, a rule to our thoughts, a bridle to our tongue, a restraint to every evil temper, then, some will say, "We may safely be dismissed from the drudgery of prayer; it will then have answered all the ends which you so tiresomely recommend." So far from it, we really figure to ourselves, that if we could hope to hear of a human being brought to such perfection of discipline, it would unquestionably be found that this would be the very being who would continue most perseveringly in the practice of that devotion, which had so materially contributed to bring his heart and mind into so desirable a state, who would most tremble to discontinue prayer, who would be most appalled at the thought of the condition into which such discontinuance would be likely to reduce him. Whatever others do, he will continue forever to "sing praises unto Thee, O Thou most Highest"; he will continue to tell of "Thy loving kindness early in the morning, and of Thy truth in the night season."

It is true that while he considered religion as something nominal and ceremonial, rather than as a principle of spirit and of life, he felt nothing encouraging, nothing refreshing, nothing delightful in prayer. But since he began to feel it as the means of procuring the most substantial blessings to his heart; since he began to experience something of the realization of the promises to his soul, in the performance of this exercise, he finds there is no employment so satisfactory, none that his mind can so little do without; none that so effectually raises him above the world; none that so opens his eyes to its empty shadows; none which can make him look with so much indifference on its lying vanities; none that can so powerfully defend him against the assaults of temptation and the allurements of pleasure; none that can so sustain him under labor, so carry him through difficulties; none that can so quicken him in the practice of every virtue, and animate him in the discharge of every duty.

An additional reason why we should live in the perpetual use of prayer seems to be that our blessed Redeemer, after having given both the example and the command while on earth, condescends still to be our unceasing intercessor in heaven. Can we ever cease petitioning for ourselves when we believe that He never ceases interceding for us?

If we are so unhappy as now to find little pleasure in this holy exercise, that, however, is so far from being a reason for discontinuing it, that it affords the strongest argument for perseverance. That which was at first a form will become a pleasure. That which was a burden will become a privilege. That which we impose upon ourselves as a medicine will become necessary as an aliment and desirable as a gratification. That which is now short and superficial, will become copious and solid. The chariot wheel is warmed by its own motion. Use will make that easy which was at first painful. That which is once become easy will soon be rendered pleasant. Instead of repining at the performance we shall be unhappy at the omission. When a man recovering from sickness attempts to walk, he does not discontinue the exercise because he feels himself weak, nor even because the effort is painful. He rather redoubles his exertion. It is from his perseverance that he looks for strength. An additional turn every day diminishes his repugnance, augments his vigor, improves his spirits. That effort which was submitted to because it was salutary is continued because the feeling of renovated strength renders it delightful.

But if prayer be so exhilarating to the soul, what shall be said of praise? Praise is the only employment, we had almost said it is the only duty, in which self finds no part. In praise we go out of ourselves and think only of Him to whom we offer it. It is the most purely disinterested of all services. It is gratitude with solicitation, acknowledgment without petition. Prayer is the overflowing expression of our wants; praise, of our affections. Prayer is the language of the destitute; praise of the redeemer, sinner. If the angelic spirits offer their praise exempt from our mixture of infirmity or alloy, yet we have a motive for gratitude unknown even to the angels. They are unfallen beings; they cannot say as we can, "Worthy the Lamb, for He was slain for us." Prayer is the child of faith; praise of love. Prayer is prospective; praise takes in, in its wide range, enjoyment of present, remembrance of past, and anticipation of future blessings. Prayer points the only way to heaven; "praise is already there."

Chapter XII

On Intercessory Prayer

As it is the effect of prayer to *expand* the affections as well as to *sanctify* them, the benevolent Christian is not satisfied to commend himself alone to the divine favor. The heart which is full of the love of God will overflow with love to his neighbor. All that are near to himself he wishes to bring near to God. He will present the whole human race as objects of the divine compassion, but especially the faithful followers of Jesus Christ. Religion makes a man so liberal of soul that he cannot endure to restrict anything, much less divine mercies, to himself. He therefore spiritualizes the social affections by adding intercessory to personal prayer, for he knows that petitioning for others is one of the best methods of exercising and enlarging our own love and charity, even if it were not to draw down those blessings which are promised to those for whom we ask them.

It is unnecessary to produce any of the numberless instances, with which Scripture abounds, on the efficacy of intercession, in which God has proved the truth of His own assurance that "His ear was open to their cry." I shall confine myself to a few observations on the benefits it brings to him who offers it. When we pray for the objects of our dearest regard, it purifies passion and exalts love into religion. When we pray for those with whom we have worldly intercourse, it smooths down the swellings of envy and bids the tumult of anger and ambition subside. When we pray for our country, it sanctifies patriotism. When we pray for those in authority, it adds a divine motive to human obedience.

When we pray for our enemies, it softens the savageness of war and mollifies hatred into tenderness, and resentment into sorrow. There is no such softener of animosity, no such soother of resentment, no such allayer of hatred as sincere cordial prayer. And we can only learn the duty so difficult to human nature of forgiving those who have offended us, when we bring ourselves to pray for them to Him whom we ourselves daily offend. When those who are the faithful followers of the same divine Master pray for each other, the reciprocal intercession delightfully realizes that beautiful idea of "the communion of Saints." There is scarcely anything which more enriches the Christian than the circulation of this holy commerce; than the comfort of believing, while he is praying for his Christian friends, that he is also repaying the benefit of their prayers for him.

Some are for confining their intercessions only to the good, as if none but persons of merit were entitled to our prayer. Good! Who is good? "There is none good but one, that is God." Merit! Who has it? Desert! Who can plead it in the sight of God? Who shall bring his own piety, or the piety of others, in the way of *claim* before a Being of such transcendent holiness that "the heavens are not clean in His sight"? And if we wait for perfect holiness as a preliminary prayer, when shall such erring creatures pray at *all* to Him "who chargeth the angels with folly"?

The social affections were given us not only for the kindliest, but the noblest purposes. The charities of father, son, and brother were bestowed not only to make life pleasant, but to make it useful; not only that we might contribute to the present comfort, but to the eternal benefit of each other.

These heaven-implanted affections are never brought into exercise more properly, nor with more lively feelings, than in intercessory prayer. Our friends may have wants which we cannot remove, desires which we cannot gratify, afflictions which we cannot relieve, but it is always in our power to bring them before God, to pray for them whenever we pray for ourselves. This, as it is a most pleasant and easy, so it is an indispensable obligation. It is a duty which brings the social affections into their highest exercise and which may be reciprocally paid and received.

The same Scriptures which expressly enjoin that application, prayers, intercession, and giving of thanks be made for all men, furnish also numerous examples of the efficacy of intercessory prayer. We need not dwell on the instance of the rain obtained by the prayers of Elijah or the earlier availing intercessions of Moses with other public deliverances effected in the same manner.

Though the perseverance of Abraham's prayer did not prevent the extermination of the polluted city, yet doubtless the blessing he solicited for it returned unto his own bosom, and the successive promises made by the Almighty Judge to the successively reduced number of the righteous, for whose sake the petition for preservation was offered, affords a proof of the divine approbation and a striking encouragement to persist in the duty of intercessory prayer. The promise of God was withdrawn. The prayer was conditional, and could the petitioner have made up his very lowest compliment, the city had been saved. The interceding heart in any event is sure to gain something for itself.

Prayer is such an enlarger of the affections, such an opener of the heart that we cannot but wonder how any who live in the practice of it should be penurious in their alms, or if they do give, should do it "grudgingly or of necessity." Surely if our prayer be cordial, we shall be more ready to assist as well as to love those for whom we are in the habit of making supplication to God. It is impossible to pray sincerely for the well-being of others without being desirous of contributing to it. We can hardly conceive a more complete species of self-deception than that practised by an avaricious professor of religion, one who goes on mechanically to pray for the poor while his prayer has neither opened his heart nor his purse. He may value himself on this, as on other instances of his ingenuity, in having found out so cheap a way of doing good, and go on contentedly till he hears that tremendous sentence of exclusion: "Inasmuch as ye did it not to one of the least of these, ye did it not to Me."

> O impudence of Wealth! with all thy store,
> How dar'st thou let one worthy man be poor?

O you great ones of the earth, whom riches ensnare and prosperity betrays, be largely liberal, even from self-interest. Not, indeed, expecting to make the liberality you bestow a remuneration for the devotions you withhold. Scatter your superfluities, and more than your superfluities, to the destitute, if not to vindicate Providence, yet to benefit yourselves. Not, indeed, to revive the old pious fraud of depending for salvation on the prayers of others, yet still you may hope to be repaid, with usurious interest, from the pious poor, by the very tender charity of their prayers for you. Their supplications may possibly be so heard that you may at length be brought to the indispensable necessity and the bounden duty of praying for yourselves.

There is a generosity in religion. The same principle which disposes a Christian to contribute to the temporal interests of those he loves inclines him to breathe his earnest supplication for their spiritual benefit.

But our intercession must neither dwell in generalities for the public nor in limitations to the wants of our particular friends. The Christian is the friend of every description of the children of mortality. In the fullness of our compassion for the miseries of mankind, we pour out our hearts in prayer for the poor and destitute, and we do well. But there is another and a large class who are still more the objects of our pity and consequently should be of our prayers. While we pray for those who have no portion in this world, do we not sometimes forget to pray for those who have their whole portion in it? We pray for the praying servants of God, but perhaps we neglect to pray for those who never pray for themselves. These are the persons who stand most in need of the mercy of the Almighty and of our Christian importunity in their favor.

Is it not affecting that even unto our devotions we are disposed to carry the regard we too highly indulge of the good things of this life, by earnestly imploring mercy upon those who want them; and by forgetting to offer our supplications in favor of those who are blinded to the too full enjoyment of them. If the one duty be done, should the other be left undone?

If we want an example of the most sublime kind of Charity, observe for what it is that the great apostle of the Gentiles "bows his knees to God" in behalf of his friends. Is it for an increase of their wealth, their power, their fame, or any other external prosperity? No. It is that "God would grant them according to the riches of His glory, to be strengthened with might in the inner-man." It is "that Christ may dwell in their hearts by faith." It is that "they may rooted and grounded in love," and this to a glorious end: "that they may be able with all Saints, to comprehend" the vast dimensions of the love of Christ, that "they may be filled with all the fullness of God." These are the sort of petitions which we need never hesitate to present. These are requests which we may rest assured are always agreeable to the divine will; here we are certain we cannot "pray amiss." These are intercessions of which the benefit may be felt, when wealth and fame and power shall be forgotten things.

Why does Saint Paul "pray day and night" that he might see the face of his Thessalonian converts? Not merely that he might have the gratification of once more beholding those he loved, though that would sensibly delight so affectionate a heart, but "that he might perfect that which was lacking in their faith."

These are instances of a spirit so large in its affections, so high in its object, of a man who had so much of heaven in his friendships, so much of soul in his attachments, that he thought time too brief, earth too scanty, worldly blessings too low to enter deeply into his petitions for those to whom time and earth, the transitory blessings of life, and life itself, would so soon be no more.

In exciting us to perpetual gratitude, the same apostle stirs us up to the duty of keeping before our eyes the mercies which so peremptorily demand it. These mercies succeed each other so rapidly, or rather are crowded upon us so simultaneously, that if we do not count them as they are received and record them as they are enjoined, their very multitude, which ought to penetrate the heart more deeply, will cause them to slip out of the memory.

As to the commanded duty of praying for our enemies, the most powerful example bequeathed to us in Scriptures, next to that of his divine Master on the cross, is that of Saint Stephen. Even *after* the expiring martyr had ejaculated, "Lord Jesus, receive my spirit," he kneeled down and cried with a loud voice, "Lord, lay not this sin to their charge." Let every instance of Roman greatness of mind, let every story of Grecian magnanimity be ransacked and produce (who can?) such another example. Theirs is tumor; this is grandeur. Theirs is heroism; this is Christianity. They implored the gods for themselves; Stephen for his murderers.

In closing the subject of Intercessory Prayer, may the author be allowed to avail herself of the feeling it suggests to her own heart; and while she earnestly implores that Being who can make the meanest of His creatures instrumental to His glory, to bless this humble attempt to the reader, may she, without presumption, entreat that this work of Christian charity may be reciprocal and that those who peruse these pages may put up a petition for her that, in the great day to which we are all hastening and to which she is so very near, she may not be found to have suggested to others what she herself did not believe or to have recommended what she did not desire to practice? In that awful day of everlasting decision, may both the reader and the writer be pardoned and accepted "not for any works of righteousness which they have done," but through the merits of the Great Intercessor.

Chapter XIII

The Practical Results of Prayer Exhibited in the Life of the Christian in the World

As the keeping up a due sense of religion, both in faith and practice, so materially depends on the habit of fervent and heartfelt devotion, may we be permitted, in this place, to insist on the probable effects which would follow the devout and conscientious exercise of prayer, rather than on prayer itself?

As soon as religion is really become the earnest desire of our hearts, it will inevitably become the great business of our lives; the one is the only satisfactory evidence of the other. Consequently, the religion of the heart and life will promote that Spirit of prayer by which both have been promoted.

They, therefore, little advance the true interest of mankind, who, under the powerful plea of what great things God has done for us in our redemption by His Son, neglect to encourage our active services in His cause. Hear the words of inspiration: "Be not slothful"; "run the race"; "fight the good fight"; "strive to enter in"; "give diligence"; "work out your own salvation"; "God is not unmindful to forget your labor of love"; "but when ye have done all ye are unprofitable servants, ye have done that which was your duty to do."

But if, after we have done all, we are unprofitable servants, what shall we be if we have done nothing? Is it not obvious that the Holy Spirit, who dictated these exhortations, clearly meant that a sound faith in the Word of God was intended to produce holy exertion for the advancement of His glory? The activity in doing good of the Son of God was not exceeded by His devotion, and both powerfully illustrated His doctrines and confirmed His divinity. Until, then, we make our religion a part of our common life; until we bring Christianity, as an illustrious genius is said to have brought philosophy, from its retreat to live in the world and dwell among men; until we have brought it from the closet to the active scene, from the church to the world, whether that world be the court, the senate, the exchange, the public offices, the private counting-house, the courts of justice, the professional departments, or the domestic drawing-room, it will not have fully accomplished what it was sent on earth to do.

We do not mean the introduction of its language, but of its spirit; the former is frequently as incompatible with public, as it is unsuitable to private business, but the latter is of universal application. We mean that the temper and dispositions which it is the object of prayer to communicate, should be kept alive in society and brought into action in its affairs. That the integrity, the veracity, the justice, the purity, the liberality, the watchfulness over ourselves, the candor toward others, all exercised in the fear of the Lord and strengthened by the Word of God and prayer, should be brought from the retirement of devotion to the regulation of the conduct.

There may be a form of unfelt petitions, a ceremonious avowal of faith, a customary profession of repentance, a general acknowledgment of sin, uttered from the lips to God; but where is His image and superscription written upon the heart? Where is the transforming power of religion in the life? Where is the living transcript of the divine original? Where is that holiness to which the vision of the Lord is specifically promised? Where is the light and life and grace of the Redeemer exhibited in the temper and conduct?

Yet we are assured that if we are Christians, there must be a constant aim at this conformity.

We should therefore endeavor to believe as we pray, to think as we pray, to feel as we pray, and to act as we pray. Prayer must not be a solitary, independent exercise, but an exercise incorporated with many, and inseparably connected with that golden chain of Christian duties, of which, when so connected, it forms one of the most important links. *They* will not *pray* differently from the rest of the world, who do not *live* differently.

But though we must not, in accommodation to the prevailing prejudices and unnecessary zeal against abstinence and devotion, neglect the imperative duties of retirement, prayer, and meditation; yet perhaps as prayer makes so indispensable an article in the Christian life, some retired contemplative persons may apprehend that it makes the whole, whereas prayer is only the operation which sets the machine going. It is the sharpest spur to virtuous action, but not the act itself. The only infallible incentive to a useful life, but not a substitute for that usefulness. Religion keeps her children in full employment. It finds them work for every day in the week, as well as on Sundays.

The praying Christian, on going into the world, feels that his social and religious duties are happily comprised in one brief sentence: "I will *think* upon Thy commandments to do them." What the Holy Spirit has so indissolubly joined, He does not separate.

As the lawyer has his compendium of cases and precedents, the legislator his statutes, the soldier his book of tactics, and every other professor his *vade mecum* to consult in difficulties, the Christian, to whichever of the professions he may belong, will take his morning lecture from a more infallible directory, comprehending not only cases and precedents but abounding with those seminal principles which entertain the essence of all actual duty, from which all practical evidence is deducible. This spirit of laws differs from all other legal institutes, some of which, from that imperfection inseparable from the best human things, have been found unintelligible, some impracticable, and some have become obsolete. The divine law is subject to no such disadvantages. It is perfect in its nature, intelligible in its construction, and eternal in its obligation.

This sacred institute he will consult in the spirit of prayer, not occasionally, but daily. Unreminded of general duty, unfurnished with some leading hint for the particular demand, he will not venture to rush into the bustle, trial, and temptation of the day. Of this aid he will possess himself with the more ease and less loss of time, as he will not have to ransack a multiplicity of folios for a detached case or an individual intricacy; for though he may not find in the Bible specific instances, yet he will discover in every page some governing truth, some rule of universal application, the spirit of which may be brought to bear on almost every circumstance, some principle suited to every purpose and competent to the solution of every moral difficulty.

Scripture does not, indeed, pretend to include technical or professional peculiarities, but it exhibits the temper and the conduit which may be made applicable to the special concerns of every man, whatever be his occupation. He will find in it the rigid direction to the right pursuit, the straight road to the proper end, the duty of a pure intention, and the prohibition of false measures to attain even a laudable object. No hurry or engagement will ever make him lose sight of that sacred aphorism, so pointedly addressed to men of business: "He that *maketh haste* to be rich shall hardly be innocent." The cautionary texts which he admired in his closet, he will not treasure up as classical mottos to amuse his fancy or embellish his discourse, but will adopt as rules of conduct and bring them into every worldly transaction, whether commercial, forensic, medical, military, or whatever else be his professed object. He will not adjust his scale of duty by the false standard of the world, nor by any measure of his own devising. He has but one standard of judging, but one measure of conduct: the infallible Word of God. This rule he will take as he finds it; he will use as he is commanded. He will not bend it to his own convenience; he will not accommodate it to his own views, his own passions, his own emolument, his own reputation.

He whose heart has been set in motion by prayer, who has had his spiritual pulse quickened by a serious perusal of the Holy Scriptures, will find his work growing upon him in regular proportion to his willingness to do it. He is diligently exact in the immediate duties of the passing day. Though procrastination is treated by many as a light evil, he studiously avoids it because he has felt its mischiefs. He is active even from the love of ease, for he knows that the duties which would have cost him little if done on the day they were due, may, by the accumulation of many neglected days, cost him much. The fear of this rouses him to immediate exertion. If the case in question be doubtful, he deliberates, he inquires, he prays. If it be clear and pressing, what his hand finds to do, he does with all his might, and in the calls of distress he always acts on his favorite aphorism: that giving soon is giving twice.

Abroad how many duties meet him! He has on his hands the poor who want bread, the afflicted who want comfort, the distressed who want counsel, the ignorant who want teaching, the depressed who want soothing. At home he has his family to watch over. He has to give instruction to his children and an example to his servants. But his more immediate as well as more difficult work is with himself, and he knows that this exercise, well performed, can alone enable him wisely to perform the rest. Here he finds work for every faculty of his understanding, every conquest over his will, for every affection of his heart. Here his spirit truly labors. He prays fervently, but he has to watch as well as to pray that his conscience be not darkened by prejudice; that his bad qualities do not assume the shape of virtues, nor his good ones engender self-applause; that his best intentions do not mislead his judgment; that his candor does not degenerate into indifference, nor his strictness into bigotry; that his moderation does not freeze, nor his zeal burn. He has to control his impatience at the defeat of his most wisely conceived plans. He will find that in his best services there is something that is wrong, much that is wanting; and he feels that whatever in them is right, is not his own, but the gift of God.

Is your Christian, then, perfect? you will perhaps ask. Ask himself. With deep and sincere self-abasement he will answer in the negative. He will not only confess more failings than even his accusers ascribe to him, but he will own what they do not always charge him with: sins. He will acknowledge that there is no natural difference between himself and his censurer, but that through divine grace, the one prays and struggles against those corruptions, the very existence of which the other does not suspect.

There is nothing more humbling to the confirmed praying Christian than that while in his happier moments he is able to figure to himself a cheering image of the glory of the Redeemer, the blessedness of the redeemed, the beauty of Christian perfection; to feel himself not only awakened, but exalted; not merely enlightened, but kindled, almost possessing, rather than anticipating heaven—while he is enabled, in a joyful measure, to meditate upon these things, to feel his mind ennobled, and his soul expanded by the contemplation, yet to find how soon the bright ideas fade, the strong impression is effaced, the heavenly vision vanished. He mourns to reflect that he does not more abidingly possess in his heart, that he does not more powerfully exhibit in his conversion, more forcibly display in his life, that spirit of which his mind has been sometimes so full, his heart so enamored, when prostrate before his Maker.

To his grief he finds that his most perfect obedience is incomplete, that his warmest affections are often languid, perhaps his best intentions not realized, the best resolves not followed up. In this view, though he is abased in dust and ashes in looking up to God as the fountain of perfection, he is cheered in looking up to Him also as the fountain of mercy in Christ Jesus. He prays as well as strives, that the knowledge of his own faults may make him more humble and his sense of the divine mercies more grateful.

But he will feel that his faith, even though it does not want sincerity, will too frequently want energy. He has, therefore, to watch against cold and heartless prayer, though perhaps the humility arising from this consciousness is a benefit in another way. He feels it difficult to bring every "thought into captivity to the obedience of Christ," yet he goes on cheerily, willing to believe that what may be difficult is not impossible. He has to struggle against over-anxiety for temporal things. He has to preserve simplicity of intention, consistency, and perseverance. He has, in short, to watch against a long list of sins, errors, and temptations which he will find heavier in weight and more in number the more closely he looks into his catalog.

The praying Christian in the world has, above all, to watch against the fear of man, as he may find it more easy to endure the cross than to despise the shame. Even if he have in a good degree conquered this temptation, he may still find a more dangerous enemy in the applause of the world than he found in its enmity. An eager desire of popularity is, perhaps, the last lingering sin which cleaves even to those who have made a considerable progress in religion, the still unextinguished passion of a mind great enough to have subdued many other passions.

The devout Christian endeavors to exemplify the emphatic description of the translated Saint in the Old Testament: "he *walks* with God." He does not merely bow down before His footstool at stated intervals. He does not ceremoniously address Him on great occasions only and then retreat and dwell at a distance. But he *walks* with Him. His habitual intercourse, his natural motion, his daily converse, his intimate communication is with his Redeemer. He is still seeking, though it may be with slow and faltering steps, the things which are above. He is still striving, though with unequal progress, for the prize of his high calling. He is still looking, though with a dim and feeble eye, for glory, honor, and immortality. He is still waiting, though not with a trust so lively as to annihilate the distance, to see his eternal redemption drawing nigh. Though his aims will always be far greater than his attainments, yet he is not discouraged. His hope is above; his heart is above; his treasure is above. No wonder, then, that his prayers are directed, and a large portion of his wealth sent forward thither, where he himself hopes soon to be. It is but transmitting his riches of both kinds, not only to his future, but his everlasting home.

The grand danger of the Christian in the world is *from* the world. He is afraid of the sleek, smooth, insinuating, and not discreditable vices. He guards against self-complacency. If his affairs prosper and his reputation stands high, he betakes himself to his only sure refuge, the throne of God, to his only sure remedy, humble prayer. He knows it is more easy to perform a hundred right deeds and to keep many virtues in exercise than "to keep himself unspotted from the world," than to hold the things of the world with a loose hand. Even his best actions, which may bring him most credit, have their dangers: they make him fear that "while he has a name to live, he is dead."

He feels that if he had no sin but vanity, the consciousness of that alone would be sufficient to set him on his guard, to quicken him in prayer, to caution him in conduct. He does not fear vanity as he fears any other individual vice, as a single enemy against which he is to be on the watch, but as that vice which, if indulged, would poison all his virtues. Among the sins of the inner man, he knows that "this kind goeth not out but by prayer." When he hears it said of any popular and, especially, of any religious character, "he is a good man, but he is vain," he says within himself, he is vain, and therefore, I fear he is not a good man. How many right qualities does vanity rob of their value, how many right actions of their reward!

Every suspicion of the first stirring of vanity in himself sends him with deeper prostration before his Maker. Lord what is man! Shall the praise of a fellow creature, whose breath is in his nostrils, whose ashes must soon be mingled with my own, which may even before my own be consigned to kindred dust—shall *his* praise be of sufficient potency to endanger the humility of a being who is not only looking forward to the applause of those glorious spirits which surround the throne of God, but to the approbation of God Himself?

When those with whom he occasionally mixes see the praying Christian calm and cheerful in society, they little suspect the frequent struggles, the secret conflicts he has within. Others see his devout and conscientious life, but he alone knows the plague of his own heart. For this plague he seeks the only remedy. To prayer, that balm of hurt minds, he constantly repairs.

The confirmed Christian will above all labor most assiduously after that *consistency of character*, which is a more unequivocal evidence of high Christian attainment, than the most prominent great qualities which are frequently counteracted by their opposites. This consistency exhibits a more striking conformity to the image of his Miker. As in the works of creation, the wisdom of the Supreme Intelligence is more admirable in the agreement and harmony of one thing with another than in the individual beauty and excellence of each. It is more conspicuous in the fitness and proportion of its parts, relatively, than in the composition of the parts themselves. By this uniformity, the results of religion are the most beautifully exhibited in the Christian character.

When we reflect on the conflicts and the trials of the conscientious, watchful, praying Christian, we shall estimate aright the value of the consoling promises of the Gospel. It is by these promises, applied through divine grace to the heart, that the Christian is gradually brought to consider prayer not merely as a duty, but to value it as a privilege. And the more earnestly he cultivates this spirit of supplication, the more deeply will it enable him to penetrate into the recesses of his own heart. The more he discovers the evils which he there finds, he will be so far from being deterred by the discovery from approaching to the fountain of mercy that it will lead him to be more diligent as well as more fervent in his application there. Nothing so faithfully reveals to us our spiritual exigencies, nothing can quicken our petitions for their relief so powerfully, as the conviction of their actual existence. In this conviction, in this earnest application, the Christian at length feels the efficacy of prayer in its consolations, its blessedness, its transforming power.

Chapter XIV

The Consolation of Prayer in Affliction, Sickness, and Death

The pagan philosophers have given many admirable precepts, both for resigning blessings and for sustaining misfortunes; but wanting the motives and sanctions of Christianity, though, they produce little practical effect. The stars which glittered in their moral night, though bright, imparted no warmth. Their most beautiful dissertations on death had no charm to extract its sting. We receive no support from their most elaborate treatises on immortality, for want of Him who "brought life and immortality to light." Their consolatory discussions could not strip the grave of its terrors, for to them it was not "swallowed up in victory." To conceive of the soul as an immortal principle without proposing a scheme for the pardon of its sins was but cold consolation. Their future state was but a happy guess; their heaven but a fortunate *conjecture.*

When we peruse their finest compositions, we admire the manner in which the medicine is administered, but we do not find it effectual for the cure, nor even for the mitigation of our disease. The beauty of the sentiment we applaud, but our heart continues to ache.

To this cold skepticism let us oppose the heart-consoling, exhilirating, triumphant *certainties* of Christianity. "I *know* that my Redeemer liveth, and that He shall stand at the latter day upon the earth. In my flesh I shall see God, whom mine eyes shall behold and not another"; "I am the resurrection and the life, saith the Lord; whosoever liveth and believeth in me shall never die." Here is the true balm of Gilead; here is the healing cordial for every human woe!

The hair-splitting casuist does not directly say that pain is not evil, but by a sophistical turn professes that philosophy will never *confess* it to be an evil. But what consolation does the sufferer draw from this quibbling nicety?

Christianity knows none of these fanciful distinctions. She never pretends to insist that pain in not an evil, but she does more: she converts it into a good. Christianity, therefore, teaches that fortitude is much more noble than philosophy, that meeting pain with resignation to the hand that inflicts it is more heroic than denying it to be an evil.

"I will be sanctified in them that draw nigh unto me," says the Almighty by His prophet. We must, therefore, when we approach Him in our devotions, frequently endeavor to warm our hearts, raise our views, and quicken our aspirations with a recollection of His glorious attributes; of that omnipotence which can give to all without the least deduction from any, or from Himself; of that ubiquity which renders Him the constant witness of our actions; of that omniscience which makes Him a discerner of our intentions and which penetrates the most secret disguises of our inmost souls; of that perfect holiness which should at once be the object of our adoration and the model of our practice; of that truth which will never forfeit any of His promises; of that faithfulness which will never forsake any that trust in Him; of that love which our innumerable offenses cannot exhaust; of that eternity which had place "before the mountains were brought forth"; of that grandeur which has set His glory above the heavens; of that longsuffering of God, who is strong and patient, and who is provoked every day; of that justice which will by no means clear the guilty, yet of that mercy which forgiveth iniquity, transgression, and sin; of that compassion which *waits* to be gracious; of that goodness which *leadeth* to repentance; of that purity which, while it hates sin, invites the sinner to return.

In seasons of distress and trial, whether from the loss of health or under whatever other afflictive dispensation he may be struggling, the Christian will endeavor to draw consolation by reviewing the mercies of his past life and anticipating the glorious promises of the life to come. If previously accustomed to unbroken health, he will bless God for the long period in which he has enjoyed it. If continued infirmity has been his portion, he will feel grateful that he has had such a long and gradual weaning from the world. From either state he will extract consolation. If pain be new, what a mercy to have hitherto escaped it! If habitual, we bear more easily what we have borne long.

He will review his temporal blessings and deliverances, his domestic comforts, his Christian friendships. Among his mercies, his now "purged eyes" will reckon his difficulties, his sorrows, and his trials. A new and heavenly light will be thrown on that passage, "It is good for me that I have been afflicted." It seems to him as if hitherto he had only heard it with the hearing of his ear, but now "his eye seeth it." If he be a real Christian and has had enemies, he will always have prayed for them, but now he will be thankful for them. He will the more earnestly implore mercy for them as instruments which have helped to fit him for his present state. He will look up with holy gratitude to the Great Physician who, by a divine chemistry in mixing up events, made that one unpalatable ingredient, at the bitterness of which he once revolted, the very means by which all things have worked *together* for good. Had they worked separately, they would not have worked efficaciously.

If our souls have been truly "sanctified by the Word of God and Prayer," we shall, under the sharpest trials, be apt to compare our own sufferings with the cup which our Redeemer drank for our sakes, drank to avert the divine displeasure from us. Let us pursue the comparative view of our condition with that of the Son of God. *He* was deserted in His most trying hour, deserted probably by those whose limbs, sight, life He had restored, whose souls He had come to save. We are surrounded by unwearied friends; every pain is mitigated by sympathy; every want not only relieved, but prevented; the "asking eye" explored; the inarticulate sound interpreted; the ill-expressed wish anticipated; the unsuspected want supplied. When *our* souls are "exceeding sorrowful," *our* friends participate in our sorrow; when desired to "watch with us," they watch, not "*one* hour," but *many*; not "falling asleep," but both flesh and spirit ready and willing; not forsaking us in our "agony," but sympathizing where they cannot relieve.

The night also will be made to the praying Christian a season of heart-searching thought and spiritual consolation. Solitude and stillness completely shut out the world, its business, its cares, is impertinences. The mind is sobered, the passions are stilled. It seems to the watchful Christian as if there were in the universe only God and his own soul. It is an inexpressible consolation to him to feel that the *one* Being in the universe who never slumbers nor sleeps is the very Being to whom he has free access even in the most unseasonable hours. The faculties of the mind may not, perhaps, be in their highest exercise, but the affections of the heart, from the exclusion of distracting objects, more readily ascend to their *noblest* object. Night and darkness are no parasites; conscience is more easily alarmed. It puts on fewer disguises. We appear to ourselves more what we really are. This detection is salutary. The glare which the cheerful daylight, business, pleasure, and company had shed over all objects is withdrawn. Schemes which in the day had appeared plausible now present objections. What had then appeared safe now at least seems to require deliberation. This silent season of self-examination is a keen detector of any latent sin which, like the fly in the box of perfume, may corrupt much that is pure.

When this communion with God can be maintained, it supplies deficiencies of devotion to those who have little leisure during the day; and by thus rescuing these otherwise lost hours, it snatches time from oblivion, at once adds to the length of life, and weans from the love of it.

If the wearied and restless body be tempted to exclaim, "Would to God it were morning!" the very term suggests the most consoling of all images. The quickened mind shoots forward beyond this vale of tears, beyond the dark valley and shadow of death; it stretches onward to the joyful morning of the Resurrection; it anticipates that blessed state where there is no more weeping and no more night; no weeping, for God's own hand shall wipe away the tears; no night, for the Lamb Himself shall be the light.

If humbling doubts of his own state depress the real penitent, what comfort may he not derive from the assurance that the acceptable sacrifice to the God of love is the troubled spirit and the broken and contrite heart?

It is a further encouragement to prayer to the dejected spirit that the Almighty was not contented to show His willingness to pardon by single declarations, however strong and full. He has heaped up words; He has crowded images; He has accumulated expressions; He has exhausted languages by all the variety of synonyms which express love, mercy, pardon, and acceptance. They are graciously crowded together, that the trembling mourner who was not sufficiently assured by one might be encouraged by another. And it is the consummation of the divine goodness that this message is not sent by His ambassador, but that the King of kings, the blessed and only Potentate, condescends Himself to pronounce this royal proclamation: "The Lord, the Lord God, merciful and gracious, longsuffering and abundant in goodness and truth, keeping mercy for thousands, forgiving iniquity, transgression, and sin!" Forgiving indeed, but in consonance with His just demand of repentance and reformation, "who will by no means clear the guilty."

Refuse not, then, to take comfort from the promises of God, when, perhaps, you are easily satisfied with the assurance of pardon from a frail and sinful creature like yourself whom you had offended. Why is God the only being who is not believed, who is not trusted? "O Thou that hearest prayer, why unto Thee will not all flesh come?"

In the extremity of pain, the Christian feels there is no consolation but in humble acquiescence in the divine will. It may be that he can pray but little, but that little will be fervent. He can articulate, perhaps, not at all, but his prayer is addressed to one who sees the heart, who can interpret its language, who requires not words, but affections. A pang endured without a murmur, or only such an involuntary groan as nature extorts and faith regrets, is itself a prayer. We have a striking instance of an answer to silent prayer in the case of Moses. In a situation of extreme distress, when he had not uttered a word, "the Lord said unto him, I have heard thy crying."

If, however, in the conduct of this nightly watching and this nightly prayer, our own stock of thought or expression be absolutely deficient, prophets and apostles will not only afford us the most encouraging examples, but the most profitable assistance. More especially the royal treasury of King David lies open to us, and whatever are our wants, there our resources are inexhaustible. The Psalms have supplied to all ages materials for Christian worship, under every supposable circumstance of human life. They have facilitated the means of negotiation for the penitent, of gratitude for the pardoned. They have provided confession for the contrite, consolation for the broken-hearted, invitation to the weary, and rest for the heavy-laden. They have furnished petitions for the needy, praise for the grateful, and adoration for all. However indigent in himself, no one can complain of want who has access to such a magazine of intellectual and spiritual wealth. These variously gifted compositions not only kindle the devoutest feelings, but suggest the aptest expressions. They invest the sublimest meanings with the noblest eloquence. They have taught the tongue of the stammerer to speak plainly. They have furnished him who was ready to perish for lack of knowledge with principles as well as feelings. They have provided the illiterate with the form, and the devout with the spirit of prayer. To him who previously felt not his wants, they have imparted fervent desires. They have inspired the faint with energy, and the naturally dead with spiritual life.

The Psalms exhibit the finest specimen of experimental and devotional religion in the world. They are attended with this singular advantage and this unspeakable comfort: that in them God speaks to us, and we speak to Him. "Seek ye My face; Thy face, Lord, will I seek." This delightful interlocution between the king of saints and the penitent sinner; this interchange of character; this mixture of prayer and promise, of help implored and grace bestowed, of weakness pleaded and strength imparted, of favor shown and gratitude returned, of prostration on one part and encouragement on the other, of abounding sorrow and overflowing mercy; this beautiful variety of affecting intercourse between sinful dust and infinite goodness lifts the abased penitent into the closest and most sublime communion with his Savior and his God.

The royal poet in these noble compositions has given us the most elevated character of prayer by showing us that supplication is the dialect of the poor in spirit; thanksgiving, the idiom of the genuine Christian; praise, his vernacular tongue.

How cheering under every species of distress to reflect that our blessed Redeemer not only suffered for us upon the cross, but is sympathizing with us now, that "in all our afflictions He is afflicted." The tenderness of the sympathy seems to add a value to the sacrifice, while the vastness of the sacrifice endears the sympathy by ennobling it.

If the intellectual powers be mercifully preserved, how many virtues may be brought into exercise on a sick bed, which had either lain dormant or been considered of inferior worth in the prosperous day of activity. The Christian temper, indeed, seems to be that part of religion which is more peculiarly to be exercised under these circumstances. The passive virtues, the least brilliant but the most difficult, are then particularly called into action. To *suffer* the whole will of God on the tedious bed of languishing is more trying than to perform the most shining exploit on the theater of the world; the hero in the field of battle has the love of fame, as well as patriotism to support him. He knows that the witnesses of his valor will be the heralds of his renown. The martyr at the stake is divinely strengthened. Extraordinary grace is imparted for extraordinary trials. His pangs are exquisite, but they are short. The crown is in sight; it is almost in possession. By faith "he sees the heavens opened." He sees the glory of God, and

Jesus standing at the right hand of God. But to be strong in faith and patient in hope in a long and lingering sickness is an example of more general use and ordinary application than even the sublime heroism of the martyr. The sickness is brought home to our own feelings. We see it with our eyes. We apply it to our hearts. Of the martyr, we read, indeed, with astonishment: our faith is strengthened and our admiration kindled. But we read it without that special appropriation, without that peculiar reference to our own circumstances which we feel in cases that are likely to apply to ourselves. With the dying friend, we have not only a feeling of pious tenderness, but here is also a community of interests. The certain conviction that his case must soon be our own makes it our own now. Self mixes with the social feeling, and the Christian death we are contemplating, we do not so much admire as a prodigy as propose for a model. To the martyr's stake we feel that we are not likely to be brought. To the dying bed we must inevitably come.

Accommodating his state of mind to the nature of his disease, the dying Christian will derive consolation in any case, either from thinking how forcibly a sudden sickness breaks the chain which binds him to the world or how gently a gradual decay unties it. He will feel and acknowledge the necessity of all he suffers to wean him from life. He will admire the divine goodness which commissions the infirmities of sickness to divest the world of its enchantments and to strip death of some of its most formidable terrors. He feels with how much less reluctance we quit a body exhausted by suffering than one in the vigor of health.

Sickness, instead of narrowing the heart, its worst effects on an unrenewed mind, enlarges his. He earnestly exhorts those around him to defer no act of repentance, no labor of love, no deed of justice, no work of mercy, to that state of incapacity in which he now lies.

How many motives has the Christian to restrain his murmurs! Murmuring offends God, both as it is injurious to his goodness and as it perverts the occasion which God has now afforded for giving an example of patience. Let us not complain that we have nothing to do in sickness when we are furnished with the opportunity as well as called to the duty of resignation. The duty, indeed is always ours, but the occasion is now more eminently given. Let us not say, even in this depressed state, that we have nothing to be thankful for. If sleep be afforded, let us acknowledge the blessing. If wearisome nights be our portion, let us remember they are "appointed to us." Let us mitigate the grievance of watchfulness by considering it as a sort of prolongation of life, as the gift of more minutes granted for meditation and prayer. If we are not able to employ it to either of these purposes, there is a fresh occasion for exercising that resignation which will be accepted for both.

If reason be still continued, yet with sufferings too intense for any devotional duty, the sick Christian may take comfort that the business of life was accomplished before the sickness began. He will not be terrified if duties are superseded, if means are at an end, for he has nothing to do but to die. This is the act for which all other acts, all other duties, all other means will have been preparing him. He who has long been habituated to look death in the face, who has often anticipated the agonies of dissolving nature, who has accustomed himself to pray for support under them, will now feel the blessed effect of those petitions which have been long treasured in heaven. To those anticipatory prayers he may, perhaps, now owe the humble confidence of hope in this inevitable hour. Habituated to the contemplation, he will not, at least, have the dreadful addition of surprise and novelty to aggravate the trying scene. It has long been familiar to his mind, though hitherto it could only operate with the inferior force of a picture to a reality. He will not, however, have so much scared his imagination by the terrors of death as invigorated his spirit by looking beyond them to the blessedness which follows. Faith will not so much dwell on the opening grave as shoot forward to the glories to which it leads. The hopes of heaven will soften the pangs which lie in the way to it. On heaven, then, he will fix his eyes, rather than on the awful intervening circumstances. He will not dwell on the struggle which is for a moment, but on the crown which is forever. He will endeavor to think less of death than of its conqueror; less of the grave than of its spoiler; less of the body in ruins than of the spirit in glory; less of the darkness of his closing day than of the opening dawn of immortality. In some brighter drawing nigh, as if the freed spirit had already burst its prison walls, as if the manumission had actually taken place, he is ready exultingly to exclaim, "My soul is escaped; the snare is broken; and I am delivered."

Eternal things now assume their proper magnitude, for he beholds them in the true point of vision. He has ceased to lean on the world, for he has found it both a reed and a spear. It has failed and it has pierced him. He leans not on himself, for he has long known his own weakness. He leans not on his virtues, for his renewed mind has shown him that they can do nothing for him. Had he no better refuge, he feels that his sun would set in darkness, his life close in despair.

He suffers not his thoughts to dwell on life. His retrospections are at an end. His prospects as to this world are at end also. He commits himself unreservedly to his heavenly Father. But though secure of the port, he may still dread the passage. The Christian will rejoice that his rest is at hand; the man may shudder at the unknown transit. If faith is strong, nature is weak. Nay, in this awful exigency, strong faith is sometimes rendered faint through the weakness of nature.

At the moment when his faith is looking round for every additional confirmation, he may rejoice in those blessed certainties, those glorious realizations which Scripture affords. He may take comfort that the strongest attestations given by the apostles to the reality of the heavenly state were not conjectural. They, to use the words of our Savior, spoke what they knew and testified what they had seen. "I reckon," says Saint Paul, "that the afflictions of this present life are not worthy to be compared with the glory that shall be revealed." He said this *after* he had been caught up into the third heaven, *after* he had beheld the glories to which he alludes. The author of the apocalyptic vision having described the ineffable glories of the New Jerusalem, thus puts new life and power into his description: "I, John, *saw* these things and *heard* them."

The power of distinguishing objects increases with our approach to them. The Christian feels that he is entering on a state where every care will cease, every fear vanish, every desire be fulfilled, every sin be done away, every grace perfected; where there will be no more temptations to resist, no more passions to subdue, no more insensibility to mercies, no more deadness in service, no more wandering in prayer, no more sorrow to be felt for himself nor tears to be shed for others. He is going where his devotion will be without langor; his life without alloy; his doubts, certainty; his expectation, enjoyment; his hope, fruition. All will be perfect, for God will be all in all.

The period at length arrives when we must summon all the fortitude of the rational being, all the resignation of the devout Christian. The principles we have been learning, the prayers we have uttered must now be made practical. The speculations we have admired, we must now realize. All that we have been studying was in order to furnish materials for this grand exigency. All the strength we have been collecting must now be brought into action. We must now draw to a point all the scattered arguments, all the several motives, all the individual supports, all the cheering promises of Christianity. We must exemplify all the rules we have given to others. We must embody all the resolutions we have formed for ourselves. We must reduce our precepts to experience. We must pass from discourses on submission to its exercise, from dissertations on suffering to sustaining it. We must heroically call up the determination of our better days. We must recollect what we have said of the supporters of faith and hope when our strength was in full vigor, when our heart was at ease and our mind undisturbed. Let us collect all that remains to us of mental strength. Let us implore the aid of holy hope and fervent faith to show that religion is not a beautiful theory, but a soul-sustaining truth.

Let us endeavor, without harassing scrutiny or distressing doubt, to act on the principles which our sounder judgment formerly admitted. The strongest faith is wanted in the hardest trials. Under those trials, to the confirmed Christian, the highest degree of grace is commonly imparted. Let us not impair that faith on which we rested when our mind was strong by suspecting its validity now it is weak. That which had our full assent in perfect health, which was then firmly rooted in our spirit and grounded in our understanding, must not be unfixed by the doubts of an enfeebled reason and the scruples of an impaired judgment. We may not be able to determine on the reasonableness of propositions, but we may derive strong consolation from conclusions which were once fully established in our mind.

Even if prayer were as worthless, with respect to present advantages, and religion as burdensome as some suppose, it would be a sufficient vindication of both that they lead to eternal bliss. Of the precise nature of that bliss, the Scripture account is calculated rather to quicken faith than gratify curiosity. There the appropriate promises to spiritual beings are purely spiritual. It is enough for believers to know that they shall be forever with the Lord; and though it does not yet appear what we shall be, yet we know that when He shall appear, we shall be like Him. In the vision of the Supreme Good, there must be supreme felicity. Our capacities of knowledge and happiness shall be commensurate with our duration. On earth, part of our enjoyment (a most fallacious part) consists in framing new objects for our wishes. In heaven there shall remain in us no such disquieting desires, for all which can be found we shall find in God. We shall not know our Redeemer by the hearing of the ear, but we shall see Him as He is. Our knowledge, therefore, will be clear because it will be intuitive.

It is a glorious part of the promised bliss that the book of prophecy shall be realized; the book of providence displayed; every mysterious dispensation unfolded, not by conjecture, but by vision. In the grand general view of Revelation, minute description would be below our ideas; circumstantial details would be disparaging; they would debase what they pretend to exalt. Those sublime negatives—"Eye hath not seen, nor ear heard, neither have entered into the heart of man, the things which God hath prepared for them that love Him"—fill the soul with loftier conceptions of eternal joys than all the elaborate but degrading delineations which have been sometimes attempted. We cannot conceive the blessings prepared for us until He who has prepared reveal them.

If, indeed, the blessedness of the eternal world could be described, new faculties must be given us to comprehend it. If it could be conceived, its glories would be lowered and our admiring wonder diminished. The wealth that can be counted has bounds. The blessings that can be calculated have limits. We now rejoice in the expectation of happiness inconceivable. To have conveyed it to our full apprehension, our conceptions, it must then be taken from something with which we are already acquainted, and we should be sure to depreciate the value of things unseen by a comparison with even the best of the things which are seen. In short, if the state of heaven were attempted to be let down to human intelligence, it would be far inferior to the glorious but indistinct glimpses which we now catch from the oracles of God, of joy unspeakable, and full of glory. What Christian does not exult in the grand outline of unknown, unimagined, yet consummate bliss: in Thy presence is the fullness of joy, and at *Thy* right hand are pleasures for evermore?